UNFUCK

USING SCIENCE TO GET OVER ANXIETY, DEPRESSION, ANGER, FREAK-OUTS, AND TRIGGERS

FAITH HARPER, PHD, LPC-S, ACS, ACN

SANAGE
PUBLISHING HOUSE

First published in India

SANAGE
PUBLISHING HOUSE

Sanage Publishing House

UNFUCK YOUR BRAIN

Using Science to Get Over Anxiety, Depression, Anger, Freak-outs, and Triggers

© Faith Harper, 2017, 2022
This Edition © Microcosm Publishing 2017
Fourteenth printing, 20,000 copies
ISBN 978-9-39411-281-0 (Paperback)

Cover by Kelly Fry
Design by Joe Biel
Illustrations on page 14, 85, 94, 156 by Joe Biel
Illustration on page 174 by Nate Powell
Illustrations on inside covers, pages 140, 172 by River Katz
Illustrations on page 90, 112 by Meggyn Pomerleau

Microcosm Publishing
2752 N Williams Ave.
Portland, OR 97227
www.Microcosm.Pub

Did you know that you can buy our books directly from us at sliding scale rates? Support a small, independent publisher and pay less than Amazon's price at www.Microcosm.Pub

To join the ranks of high-class stores that feature Microcosm titles, talk to your local rep: In the U.S. **Como** (Atlantic), **Fujii** (Midwest), **Book Travelers West** (Pacific), **Turnaround** in Europe, **UTP/Manda** in Canada, **New South** in Australia, and **GPS** in Asia, Africa, India, South America, and other countries. We are sold by **Faire** in the gift market.

Library of Congress Cataloging-in-Publication Data

Names: Harper, Faith G., author.
Title: Unfuck your brain : using science to get over anxiety, depression,
    anger, freak-outs, and triggers / Faith G. Harper, PhD, LPC-S, ACS.
Description: First edition. | Portland, OR : Microcosm Publishing, [2017]
Identifiers: LCCN 2016048189 (print) | LCCN 2017006804 (ebook) | ISBN 9781934620779 (pbk.) |
ISBN 9781621060208 (epdf) | ISBN 9781621060406 (epub) | ISBN 9781621064978 (mobi/kindle)
Subjects: LCSH: Psychic trauma--Treatment--Popular works. | Stress
    management. | Mental health. | Psychotherapy.
Classification: LCC RC552.T7 H365 2017 (print) | LCC RC552.T7 (ebook) | DDC 616.85/21--dc23
LC record available at https://lccn.loc.gov/2016048189

Microcosm Publishing is Portland's most diversified publishing house and distributor with a focus on the colorful, authentic, and empowering. Our books and zines have put your power in your hands since 1996, equipping readers to make positive changes in your life and in the world around you. Microcosm emphasizes skill-building, showing hidden histories, and fostering creativity through challenging conventional publishing wisdom. What was once a distro and record label was started by Joe Biel in his bedroom and has become among the oldest independent publishing houses in Portland, OR. In a world that has inched to the right for 80 years, we are carving out a place in the center with DIY skills, food, bicycling, gender, self-care, and social justice.

Global labor conditions are bad, and our roots in industrial Cleveland in the 70s and 80s made us appreciate the need to treat workers right. Therefore, our books are MADE IN THE USA and printed on post-consumer paper.

CONTENTS

INTRODUCTION

How do our brains get fucked up? Let us count the ways.

Anger, depression, anxiety, stress, traumatic grief, substance use, crazy-ass behavioral patterns, dumb-ass relationship choices.

Or as someone said to me recently... "Yeah, that's just a typical Tuesday."

So much of what we call mental illness is really a case of brain chemicals gone batshit. And most of this comes from the stressful and traumatic life events we cope with.

We used to hold our poor genes accountable for all the different ways we responded to an environment of stress and trauma. But recent research shows that only two to five percent of the diagnoses people struggle with come from a singular, faulty gene. So we know that the cause of trouble is waaaaaaay more likely to be our environment and how we cope with it.

These things—anger, depression, the rest of it—are **adaptive strategies.** If you don't believe anything else I have to say, I hope you believe this part. These feelings are normal. We're wired for self-protection and survival, and that's exactly what your brain is doing when it's acting all fucked up.

Our behaviors are responses to the bullshit we have to deal with day in and day out. Our brains respond not just to big, life altering traumatic events but also to day to day toxic relationships and interactions...the small ways people push our buttons, violate our boundaries, and disrespect our need for safety. It's a hot mess combination of the two.

And THEN feeling fucked up becomes a vicious cycle. We feel weird and crazy for feeling weird and crazy. We feel like we are weak. Or broken. Or fundamentally flawed. And *that* is the most helpless feeling in the world. Fundamentally flawed means un-fixable. So why bother trying?

But what if you could understand where all of those thoughts and feelings are coming from? And understand how all the shit going on in your head came to be? What if it were actually entirely understandable? That means it might actually be FIXABLE.

This is important shit. We are way more likely to get better if we know why we are having a certain problem rather than just focusing on the symptoms. If we treat stress, anxiety, or depression, for example, without looking at some of the *causes* of the stress, anxiety, and depression, then we aren't doing everything we can to make things ACTUALLY BETTER.

It's like if you get a rash (bear with me, gross analogy, I know). You can treat the rash and maybe even make it go away, but if you don't figure out what you were allergic to? Continued issues with rashes are pretty likely.

Same with the brain. If you can understand better why you are doing the things you are doing, the getting better part gets way easier. And it doesn't have to be explained in a super-complicated fancy-pants way to make sense and be useful.

I'm a therapist. A licensed counselor with additional certifications in sexology, integrated life coaching, and clinical nutrition. I'm also a board supervisor and I teach classes all around the state. I'm a trauma-informed therapist, which means I do treat the trauma along with the rest. This does two things:

1) It means I'm actively avoided at parties
2) My clients seem to get way better, way faster than the clients of my colleagues who don't incorporate trauma work and awareness into their practice

I'm not being all self-congratulatory here. My clients do ALL the fucking work, I'm just the coach. I hold up the huge banner that says "Run this way, Forrest!" at the proper end zone.

I've been in the mental health field for enough decades now for you to say *"Damn, you're old,"* and I can tell you that our current understanding of trauma is fairly new. Several years ago I worked for a program that was the first in town to run trauma recovery groups. In those groups, I saw that focusing on working through trauma histories, rather than the labels we attached to them (depression, anxiety, addiction, etc.) helped people get better. Since that time I trained in several more trauma treatment modalities, and helped several agencies and programs move into using a trauma informed treatment model.

I'm currently working in private practice and my focus is on relationships and intimacy. Guess what the biggest issue I run into is? Trauma history. It rears its ugly head up everywhere. I found that when I explained everything that was going on in a way that was simple, my clients would say "Oh, shit! That makes sense!" This book exists because nobody else had smushed all that stuff together in a way that is simple and practical. And I have seen how understanding all this shit helps people figure out the getting better part way more quickly.

This may be bad for business, but I don't think everyone needs therapy. I hope everyone includes some kind of wellness work in their lives, but we each have to find the route that makes the most sense for us. Some people meditate, some people exercise, some people have a life coach, and some people see a therapist. Some people do something entirely different. It's all good.

Because, hey...you do you. Whatever that ends up being, I'm convinced that everything works better if you understand the why part. And the end-goal of the doing things differently, whatever that thing may be.

WHO IS THIS BOOK FOR?

This book is for the people who ask *"But, WHY?"* all the time. The people who annoyed the crap out of the adults around them when they were little kids by asking questions about how the world worked so they could understand their place in it. Because the *why* is REALLY NEEDFUL INFORMATION.

This book is for all the people who fucking HATE being told what to do by other people. Who just want the tools and the information that they need to figure out what to do for *themselves*. You may be figuring this shit out by yourself or with a rock-star therapist who knows better than to boss you around. Either way, you know you are in charge of your own fucking life when it comes down to it, because you are sure as hell responsible for all the consequences.

This book is for the people who are fucking tired of hearing or thinking that they are just crazy. Or stupid. Or lazy. Or "too sensitive." Or just need to "get over" themselves. Who are tired of feeling bad, but even more tired of other people thinking they *enjoy* feeling bad. Like anyone would choose misery. Like they think you are just refusing to get better. Like you want to be miserable. Of fucking course you don't. But you've been stuck, and with no idea why.

So this book is about the why you are miserable so you can do something about it.

WHAT IS GOING TO HAPPEN IN THIS BOOK?

So, ok. You're thinking: *That's all well and good, fancy doctor lady. How is this book going to help? What makes this book all kinds of special and different from the eleventy-billion other self-help books toppling off my bookshelves already? I'm skeptical as fuck right now.*

Word. You should be. My bookshelves are crammed full, too. I've probably read most everything you've read.

This book is different, for serious.

First up? I'm gonna lay some science on you. Not complex, dry, boring-as-a-box-of-rocks science, but *"Holy shit, that makes sense, how come no one ever explained it to me like that before???"* science.

I found in my private practice that it DOESN'T take twelve years of college and two hundred thousand dollars of student loan debt to understand this shit. I can generally explain what you need to know about what's going on with the brain in about five to ten minutes (or an equal number of written pages, as the case may be).

Second? I'm not gonna lay all this brain science shit on you and then say "Yeah, that's fucked up...sucks to be you" and walk away. I'm going to go through a lot of advice that is actually practical and doable for getting better.

Not everyone has time for an *Eat, Pray, Love* type of retreat (and clearly, I'm not at all jealous or anything). Most of us have to get up every day, deal with real life, and try to figure out the getting better part during that process. Getting better doesn't mean you don't have to keep doing your own laundry. So we are going to DIY this shit like rock stars. Because you know what? The situation isn't hopeless. YOU aren't hopeless. GETTING BETTER HAPPENS. If you were a client at my office, we would be wrestling these demons back into submission together. This is the next best thing. And it's the shit that works.

Third? I'm going to go through a lot of the treatment options out there. I'm not against medication and Western care...BUT I do believe they belong in their proper place as one of many treatment options. Holistic care means the *whole fucking person*. And we have to build a plan that works for us. For example, my best line of defense is eating healthy, being forced to exercise now and then, taking herbal supplements, and embracing acupuncture, meditation, massage, and pedicures as part of my wellness regime. And I will fight anyone *to the pain* (yes, *Princess Bride* reference) over my belief that pedicures are therapeutic. For my son, it's football, weightlifting, grounding exercises, meditation, a highly structured school environment, neurofeedback, and a combo of both supplements and Western meds. We all have unique needs. Pedicures, strangely, are not on his list. So I will throw in a lot of options you maybe haven't heard about in order to help you create your own plan of attack.

And throughout the book there will be mini-exercises that will help you process the work that you are doing. It's not homework, you don't have to pass a final exam. But having ways to process all the stuff that may come up for you is important. I'm not about to have you carrying my book around with your entrails hanging out because it eviscerated you, FFS. Don't use it if you don'tneed it. But it's there if you do.

TAKE ACTION: TAKING YOUR OWN TEMPERATURE

How often in life have you genuinely been given permission to feel what you feel? Rarely to fucking never is my bet.

This book is all about working through the types of shit that get in the way of us having the lives we want and the sense of purpose and peace that we crave. The type of bullshit we call traumatic events. It's also for people with huge stress responses, anxiety, grief, anger, depression, and/or addictive behaviors—all the coping skills we develop to get through life without trying to end it.

And that makes for stressful reading. Some paragraph in here may end up sucker punching your ass because it hits a fundamental truth about your life and experience. And your brain isn't gonna be happy with those feels. Your brain may be all *"Fuck this noise and toss that book."*

Because we are generally told not to feel negative emotions. They are bad and to be avoided. And we're going to go further into why that is complete bullshit.

But in the meantime, it can be really helpful to tap into what you're feeling. Take your own temperature, so to speak. And have an action plan for if it gets too high. You are going to learn more exercises that you can incorporate later on in this book. But let's start with the simplest first.

Shut your eyes right now and notice:

- What's going on in your body?
- What are you thinking? (It may not be actual thoughts but flashes of memory tapes playing.)

What are you feeling in response to that? Name those emotions. Rate the severity of them.
- Now what do you notice is going on physically, in your body?
- And, seriously, what other shit are you dealing with in your everyday life that's either helping you cope or making it worse?

This exercise might be really hard for you. Lots of people have no fucking clue how they feel. And that's OK, too. You've been trained to be disconnected from that. Told what you felt was wrong. That you weren't allowed.

So if you don't know...acknowledge that, too. You may find as you do this particular exercise over time, you will start connecting to what you feel again. Not knowing does NOT make you a self-help book drop-out. It's just more vital information about where you are right now.

All this exercise does is give you back your power to own what is going on inside you.

You have permission to feel what you feel.

Learning to reconnect with the reality of your experience will help you gather the resources you need to move forward. Because you deserve to. We should honor the past, we should remember it, and we should respect what it has taught us. But we don't have to keep living there. That house is crumbling and toxic and far too small to contain you. It doesn't support your present experience and it sure

PART ONE:

THIS IS YOUR BRAIN ON TRAUMA

HOW OUR BRAINS GET FUCKED

Short answer? Trauma.

This book is essentially all about **trauma**. And our traumatic responses, life bullshit, and other-people's dickitude that gets in the way of us kicking ass at life. It's also about how we create coping strategies that deal with this bullshit that fancy doctor people call anxiety, depression, addiction, anger, etc.

These strategies are essentially part of the whole complicated process of your brain responding after shit goes down in your life. The brain is really just trying to do its job by protecting you the best way it knows how. But the brain often ends up being a not-particularly-helpful asshole instead. It's like your friend that offers to beat the shit out of anyone who upsets you. Gratifying, but not helpful in the long run.

This book is also about **general life bullshittery and other-people's dickitude.** The shit that might not be traumatic, per se, but isn't making anything any easier. The ways we manage stuff that isn't full blown trauma…but sure as fuck isn't kittens, rainbows, and teddy bears. Like with trauma, the coping skills we create for THESE situations tend to be less and less useful over time and downright exhausting.

The good news is, no matter how long you've been stuck in this quicksand, you CAN rewire your response and unfuck your brain.

WHY IS MY BRAIN A BIG, HOT MESS?

We have a tendency to separate mental health from physical health. As if they don't affect each other in a *continuous fucking feedback loop*, or something.

Stuff we learn about the brain itself generally falls under the "physical health" category. Thoughts, feelings, and behaviors fall under the "mental health" category.

So where does this thinking and feeling fit in our body? Our mind seems to be this helium balloon floating over our heads at all times. We are holding on to the string, maybe, but it isn't really part of us (though we are still held accountable for all of it).

That image of a disembodied brain isn't helpful. It doesn't make one bit of sense.

And what we actually know about the brain is this: it at least somewhat lives in our gut. Unique microorganisms reside there that communicate so consistently with our actual brains (through the gut-brain axis…an actual real thing) to the point that they are referred to as a second brain. One that plays a huge role in guiding our emotions. Ever had a gut reaction? Yeah, that's a real thing.

Which is to say, instead of being a thing that's barely tethered to us and gets us in trouble all the time, our mind actually lies deep in the middle of our body, acting as a control center, taking in tons of information, and making decisions before we are even aware that a decision needs to be made.

Our thoughts, feelings, and behaviors come from HERE. They are rooted deep in our physical bodies, in how our brains perceive the world around us, based on past experiences and current information. So it might be the understatement of the decade to say that knowing what's going on in your brain and how all that shit works is HUGE. And when we totally get all that, we see that how we interact with the world around us is a completely normal response when we take into account brain functioning and our past experiences. If all is bopping along and the landing is smooth, we don't notice any problems. But when we have a rough landing? When brain-traffic control doesn't manage its shit properly, we see the effects:

- Freaking the fuck out
- Avoiding important shit we need to take care of
- Feeling pissed off all the time
- Being a dick to people we care about
- Putting shit in our bodies that we know isn't good for us
- Doing shit we know is dumb or pointless or destructive

None of these things are fucking helpful. But they all make sense.

As we navigate the world, nasty shit happens. The brain stores info about the nasty shit to try to avoid it in the future. Your brain has adapted to the circumstances in your life and started doing things to protect you, bless it. Sometimes these responses are helpful. Sometimes the responses become a bigger problem than the actual problem was. Your brain isn't TRYING to fuck you over (even though sometimes it totally does).

And even if you aren't dealing with a specific trauma? Adaptive coping strategies, bad habits, and funky behaviors all wire in similar ways. And research is showing that these issues are actually some of the easier ones to treat in therapy...if we address what's really going on, rather than just the symptoms.

I have found that one of the most helpful things I do as a therapist is explain what is going on inside the brain and how the work we are doing in therapy is designed to rewire our responses to certain situations.

The strategies we work on in therapy (and the strategies and skills people figure out for themselves) are designed to wire the brain back to processing information without triggering some kind of crazy overreaction. This overreaction is our brain's way of adapting and protecting us whenever it perceives a situation as a threat...so we are prepared to do whatever we need to do to stay alive. Battle brain ACTIVATE. Even if the "enemy" is just some rando next to you at the bookstore who has no idea they just triggered you.

If we can regain control, then we can respond to these perceived threats in the safest, most rational way possible.

Lemme explain what I mean by that.

BRAIN 101

So if any part of the book is complicated, it's this part. Because brains are pretty fucking complicated. But this part will only get as complicated as absolutely necessary to explain the shit you are wanting to know about what's going on. So hang with me, we got this.

The prefrontal cortex (we'll call it the PFC), essentially the front part of your brain, is the part that is in charge of **executive functioning**, which includes problem-solving, goal-oriented behaviors, and managing social interactions according to expectations of what is "appropriate." Essentially, executive function is just straight up thinking.

It's sort of behind your forehead (which makes sense with the name, right?). This is the part of the brain that evolved the most recently, and is the part that makes us the most different from other species. This is the part of the brain that is in charge of receiving information from the world and managing our thoughts and actions accordingly.

The prefrontal cortex is also the part that takes the longest to develop as we grow up. It isn't at full capacity until we are in our mid-20s. That doesn't mean that it doesn't exist in children, adolescents, and young adults. And it sure as hell doesn't mean you have a free pass on doing stupid shit if you are younger. But it does mean all our brain wiring creates new and more complex communication networks—new pathways for communication—as we get older and wiser. And if it all goes well, the PFC continues to work better and better—a definite benefit of aging.

Hold on to that *if it all goes well* part for me, though.

So the prefrontal cortex is the part that is theoretically in charge.

And the prefrontal cortex is, understandably, highly connected to the rest of the brain. The ventral portion (which is just, you know, the *backside* of the PFC...the PFC booty, so to speak) is directly linked to an entirely different area of the brain...the part that stores emotions (more on that mess inna second). Additionally, the entire PFC receives feedback from the brainstem arousal systems (don't worry, more on that later, too).

So whatever information is being sent to the PFC from these other parts of the brain impacts that whole thinking thing. There is a region of the PFC called the anterior cingulate cortex. The job of this region is to manage the dialogue between the PFC (think-y brain) and the limbic system (feely brain). The ACC manages the convo in the brain between what we know and what we feel...and then make suggestions on what we should do about the whole mess.

And our wiring in that area is fucking WEIRD. The brain cells here are called spindle neurons...they are long, leggy supermodels instead of short and bushy like they are everywhere else. These fuckers can haul some serious ass, to boot. They send signals way faster than the rest of the neurons, so you are hit up with an emotional response fast.

Why those and why there? Only humans and great apes have spindle neurons. A lot of scientists think that they are part of our evolution to higher cognition.

In order to think more, we have to feel more. And then take both into account when making decisions. Emotions are just as important for our survival as thoughts. And you are totally seeing where I am going with this already.

THE ASSHOLE AMYGDALA

So that middle-ish part of the brain that I mentioned? The part doing the tango with the PFC booty? That's the limbic system. This portion is buried a bit in the folds of the brain, behind the PFC. If the PFC does the thinking part, the limbic system does the emotions part. And a lot of that emotions part has to do with how we store memories.

The amygdala and the hippocampus are two key parts of the limbic system. Most of what we now know about how trauma affects the brain is tied into research about the amygdala. The amygdala's job is to relate memories to emotions. True dat. But, to be more specific, the amygdala has been found to only store a *specific* kind of memory, not all of them. The amygdala doesn't give a shit where you left your car keys. The amygdala's function is to manage *episodic-autobiographical memory* (EAM). Essentially this is the storage of event-based knowledge. Times, locations, people. Not your great-aunt's banana pudding recipe. Your stories about the world and how it works. *The shit that happens to you.*

So why the fuck is this important? Episodic memories get stored in the hippocampus as our stories—our interpretation of events with our emotional responses attached to them. These are memories that are tied to serious emotional reactions. If something happened in your life that was really significant to you, the emotions tied to that memory become attached like cat hair or static cling. So when we have an emotional response in the future, the amygdala immediately pulls this EAM file in order to decide how to respond.

What fires together, wires together.

Say you got flowers. Flowers are excellent, right? Sure…if your past memories of getting flowers were happy ones. Maybe your partner gave you flowers once and then proposed. So when you're getting flowers in the future, seeing flowers, driving by a flower delivery truck? Nice feelings.

But say you got flowers when a loved one died…terribly and suddenly. Some nice person knew you were hurting and sent you flowers. But now even the smell of flowers may make you queasy.

The amygdala had turned the memory of flowers into an *actual mnemonic* for certain emotions. A mnemonic like ROY G BIV to remember the colors of the rainbow or "Every Good Boy Does Fine" to remember the note breakdown on a musical scale. Shit I've not been able to unlearn from grade school.

The amygdala's job is to make sure you don't forget things that are very important. Remembering important-good is awesome. Nobody bitches about nice memories. Constant memories of important-bad can sucketh muchly.

It sucks because the amygdala doesn't really discriminate super well, especially when it's trying to protect you. It ROY G BIVs your ass into equating flowers with death. And then you're walking down the street on a spring day and smell the flowers blooming in your neighbor's garden. And suddenly you feel like you've lost your fucking mind, because even though your body is still in your neighbor's garden, your brain is back at your loved one's funeral.

FIGHT, FLIGHT, OR FREEZE...IT'S THE BRAINSTEM!

And that brings us to the last part of our brain convo, where we talk about one final part of the brain...the brainstem.

The brainstem is the very base of the brain (makes sense, right?). It is the first part of the brain to evolve into being, and the part that attaches to the vertebrae in our neck and back. You've seen how the brain looks like a bunched up mass of overcooked pasta, right? This is the part of the brain that is starting to untangle itself from the rest of the noodles, straighten out a bit, and transition into being your spinal cord.

The brainstem is our fundamental survival tool. While cardiac muscles regulate basic needs like the *breathing in and out* and the *heart going pump pump pump* all day long, the brainstem controls the rate, speed, and intensity. So it will ramp up for a panic attack, for example. Because PAYATTENTIONWEMIGHTBEDYINGFFS. You know, the important stuff.

Being alert, being conscious, being aware of our surroundings? Brainstem tasks.

So when the brainstem is saying "OW OW OW MOTHERFUCKER" or "Danger Will Robinson!" it is actually flooding the prefrontal cortex with a bunch of neurochemicals that change how the PFC operates.

The brainstem may be a basic bitch, but it is sure as hell in charge of a lot.

When the brainstem senses danger, the behavioral actions of the prefrontal cortex become FIGHT, FLIGHT, or FREEZE.

Fight is BEAT THEIR ASS BEFORE YOUR ASS GETS BEAT.

Flight is GET THE FUCK UP OUT OF HERE THIS ISN'T SAFE.

And Freeze is IF YOU PLAY POSSUM AND DON'T RESPOND AT ALL MAYBE ALL THIS WILL GO AWAY.

Don't get me wrong...these are essential survival tasks when something dangerous is going on. They are *crazy important* to our survival. This whole process is our emergency broadcast system, replete with electronic beeping in the background.

The prefrontal cortex takes in some outside information. The amygdala says I REMEMBER THAT! LAST TIME THAT SHIT HAPPENED, IT HURT! HURT SUCKS! And the brainstem tells the prefrontal cortex GET THE FUCK UP OUT OF THERE! WE DON'T LIKE TO HURT!

So we say "Peace out, threatening situation, gotta jet!" Or we fight back. Or we freeze up and play dead and hope the situation passes us over. All kinds of things can feel threatening...like a final exam or a bullshit work deadline. But those don't need a HOLY SHITBALLS IMMA GONNA BE A DINOSAUR SNACK response. Except the brainstem evolved to avoid being a dinosaur snack and NOT to deal with bullshit traffic and people who hit the heels of our feet with their shopping carts at the grocery store (though, you could totally argue the point that they are bigger shitheads than hungry dinosaurs).

SQUISH IT ALL TOGETHER? WE GOT STORYTELLING BRAINS

We all understand this to a certain extent, I think. The idea that human beings are storytellers, that is. But only to a certain extent. Because we don't really talk about the fact that this is an actual, evolutionary function. Partially because this is pretty new research, and also because it's kinda weird, when you think about it.

We don't just tell stories because we want to...we HAVE to. It's a biological human drive. In fact, we are so wired to tell stories that we even do it in our sleep. This is why we dream.

The brain has a default mode. Everything essentially has a default mode, right? Some sort of resting state. A light switch turned off is in default mode. When you turn on the light, you activate it.

When the brain is activated, it's to concentrate on some kind of outside input. A problem to solve, someone to attend to, something that needs to be done that requires focused, conscious concentration. The rest of the time, the brain is in default mode. Awake and aware, but generally resting.

Researchers have been able to map the brain in default mode…and here is where it gets really fucking interesting. The brain in default mode is the storytelling brain.

Our brain in resting state is when we story-tell. You've totally caught yourself doing this. You're driving home. Nothing you need to attend to, you know this route so well, you aren't really engaged. Storytelling mode ACTIVATE. You're telling yourself a story about what you are going to cook for dinner, or watch on TV, or the errands you have to run. These conversations aren't bullet pointed reminder lists…you actually walk through a story of your plan.

A storytelling brain is an excellent fucking thing most of the time.

- Stories are often rehearsals for life events, which makes them really fucking useful if we are getting ready to field test a new skill.
- Stories allow us to hold larger chunks of information than we could otherwise. The PFC is designed to hold about seven pieces of information (plus or minus two). We try to juggle more than that, we start dropping things off the list. Stories, however, help us hold tons more information because they create pathways for remembering far more than we could otherwise.

- Stories are our primary mode of communication with others. According to researcher Lewis Mehl-Madrona, MD, PhD, they are the neural pathways of our collective, cultural brain. It isn't just how we hold information inside, it is how we share it outside.

But clearly the storytelling brain has the capacity to be a serious fucking problem, too. We start telling ourselves (and believing) certain stories about ourselves and the world around us. Our brains are wired to crave certainty. We WANT to see patterns in what happens so we can make better decisions about the world and how we are supposed to keep ourselves safe in it. Brains are stubborn motherfuckers that already have a story they've put together about what is real and true about the world.

You've seen that right? No matter what evidence to the contrary someone sees, they are determined as fuck to stay on course with their decision. It's why elections can be so fucking crazy. Or people lose a fortune in a casino. The emotional brain makes a decision for us and the thinking brain has to scramble to come up with a reason why.

Brains will rationalize the hell out of anything.

YES, YOU CAN RETRAIN YOUR BRAIN

Brains are adaptable little assholes, and you sure-as-fuck can retrain them. Don't believe me? Well, first of all you should. I'm a fancy doctor. But if you are one of those "Fuck your degree, I want proof!" people, go to YouTube and search for "Lumiere Brothers Arrival of a Train." It's only a 45 second clip. I'll wait here.

So picture this: Paris. 1895. These bros were photography pioneers who presented the first "moving picture" to the public at an art exhibition. They were totes excited about their project…but didn't get the expected response. Instead, the moviegoers flipped their shit, and all screamed in terror and hid under the seats. Like, every single one.

The brain's way of perceiving information was telling them all "TRAIN ABOUT TO HIT YOUR STUPID ASS, GET OFF THE TRACKS!"

Because, yeah. Trains were dangerous and moving images of trains did not exist until that point. Their brains perceived the train as a reality instead of a movie.

When you watched this, did your brain freak out? Duh, no. You know what a movie is. Your neural mechanisms have been trained to understand representational train versus literal train.

And now your brain needs to learn real danger versus perceived danger. Remember that everybody's brain has issues with differentiation, especially when it comes to survival. Like the toddler who calls all animals *doggies* until they learn that there are also *horsies*, and *kitties*, and *llamas*, and *great white sharks*. The brain is going around yelling DOGGIE DOGGIE DOGGIE all the fucking time.

That is, your brain is presuming danger until it can be convinced otherwise. The amygdala is not trusting the PFC's interpretation at the moment. The minute the PFC is thinking *"hmmm, animal?"*

the amygdala grabs the control stick away from the PFC while screaming DOOOOOOGGIEEEEEE.

That's a lot of mixed metaphor. Sorry about that. Simple version? We have to get the PFC back in charge. Give it a chance to decide if it's an actual doggie or something else. We have to convince the PFC and the amygdala to hug it out and do their respective jobs, which means working the fuck TOGETHER.

IT'S OFFICIAL. YOU ARE NOT CRAZY. A DOCTOR JUST SAID SO.

Yeah, that was a lot of shit to read about the brain, but it's important shit. Because it means that what we are doing, what we are thinking, and how we are feeling *make fucking sense.*

Whether you find yourself defensive and combative as fuck, freaking out hardcore, or completely shut off and disassociated, it's your survival mode that is responding. The problem is when this happens during situations that aren't actually life threatening emergencies. The amygdala has hijacked your ability to manage the situation in a rational way using the prefrontal cortex.

It is not a *"Hey, let's investigate this situation, have rational conversations, and then determine how we want to respond based on what will best benefit us in the long run"* kind of thinking. Your amygdala screamed "DUCK AND COVER!" and all rational responses went out the window.

Duck and cover thinking isn't a bad thing at all. It's the kind of thinking we need when we hear gunshots or tornado sirens. We want to override our executive functioning if we accidentally touch a hot stove. If we didn't, that would mean that while our hand is burning, we are going through an intellectual deconstruction of the experience while our amygdala and brainstem are screaming bloody murder in the background. This is not a postmodern piece of experimental cinema. This is LIFE. We want a brain whose job is to keep us alive, right? Not just remember our locker combination from 6th grade and all the lyrics to Taylor Swift's "Shake It Off," FFS.

But in the process, it also protects us from everything it PERCEIVES as danger, not just ACTUAL danger. Our ability to discriminate between real danger and perceived danger is an imperfect system. The brain is going to err on the side of caution, even if that means you shut down when you don't actually need to.

Say you are just trying to pick up some groceries, but walking through the floral department your brain goes "FLOWERS! ROY G BIV! ABORT MISSION!" And you are in a full blown panic attack, running out of the store before you pass out. And you still don't have any fucking groceries for dinner.

You are all *"Damn, Self, that was just the floral department. Just some carnations and roses. No one died, and now I'm stuck eating ramen noodles again."* Or maybe you are not even sure why you lost your shit and are thinking *"Damn, Self, do you have to be all 50 shades of batshit crazy?"*

That rational part? The *"just carnations and roses, simmer the fuck down"* part? That requires **stimulus discrimination.**

You know. *The ability to decide if something is actually a problem or not.*

Stimulus discrimination is a thinking thing, not an emotions thing. Which means it happens in the prefrontal cortex, and once the brainstem gets into freak-out mode, it's really hard to get the prefrontal cortex up and running again. But we can do it. And we are going to talk about how we retrain our brain to respond in ways that better suit **life as it is now** instead of **life as it was in the past.**

Our stimulus discrimination response is based on all of our past experiences and habits, and that response is even more ingrained if those experiences were traumatic ones. If a stimulus is attached to a strong memory, the body starts shooting off hormones and neurotransmitters to prepare itself for response. Brains don't really have new thoughts so much as different configurations and mash-ups of old thoughts.

This is why a military vet may freak out at seeing garbage by the side of the road, after being in Iraq and driving through areas replete with improvised explosive devices.

This is why an individual who was abused may freak out by smelling a certain scent they associate with their abuser.

The brain knows its history. It has been trained to do whatever it can to remain safe. It's creating stories about your current experience or possible future experiences based on its past information. It doesn't realize or doesn't trust that you actually ARE safe.

TAKE ACTION: TRIGGER IS NOT JUST ROY ROGERS' HORSE

We throw around the word trigger on the internetz like it's fucking confetti or something. But a trigger, in this context, just means *the cause part* of a cause-and-effect type situation thingy going on.

Sometimes we know straight up what our triggers are gonna be. For example, anxiety may be the motherfucking gremlin on your back. You may know a first date, or a public speaking engagement, or a meeting with your boss is going to send your anxiety through the roof. Or a road trip where you can't find a clean rest stop with a non-sketch bathroom is gonna cause a freak out (And why is there NOT an app for that??? The struggle is REAL).

But sometimes? Not a fucking clue. Like all other mental health issues, we may have a genetic predisposition to certain responses and/or it may be a product of the environment we grew up in or live in now. And that can make figuring out our specific triggers difficult.

Next time you start feeling yourself getting into Eject mode, ask yourself these questions. And later, when you've cooled off, write the answers down:

- What specific emotion were you feeling?
- On a 0-100% scale how would you rate that emotion?
- What were the specific symptoms you felt (your emotional *response*)?

what else was going on when it hit? Just write down everything that was going on, no matter how mundane. Because, patterns over time is how we figure out our triggers.

Another method is to keep a mood tracking diary (either an app or old school paper one). This feels like a lot of work, but can really help with figuring out your triggers until you get the hang of doing it mentally throughout your day. Here is a quick guide to how to make a mood tracker diary. You can download a printable copy from *FaithGHarper.com*:

WEEKLY MOOD TRACKER	MOOD	SITUATION	MAGNITUDE (0-100)	SYMPTOMS
SUNDAY				
MONDAY				
TUESDAY				
WEDNESDAY				
THURSDAY				
FRIDAY				
SATURDAY				

AM I IN A BAD MOOD OR... DO YOU SUCK?

HOW TRAUMA REWIRES THE BRAIN

OK, LADY, WHAT THE FUCK DO YOU MEAN BY TRAUMA?

A **trauma** is an event that happens outside our understanding of how the world is supposed to work. A **traumatic response** is when our ability to cope with what happened goes to shit and it's affecting other areas of our life.

There are lots of things that can operate as a trauma. To be honest, there are plenty of things that are deeply traumatic for many people that aren't really considered by our diagnostic manuals. It's one of the things that burns my ass, because it then leads to people feeling ashamed that their trauma wasn't traumatic enough to warrant attention. And that's some bullshit right there. Because fancy terms and definitions aside? A trauma is a "What the fuck was THAT?" situation.

A trauma can be an accident, an injury, a serious illness, a loss… **or any kind of life event that kicks your ass.**

But in the end? We all experience trauma differently, and are impacted by too many things to list. Creating a list that touches only on the big "diagnosable" categories dismisses other experiences that shouldn't be dismissed.

By one estimate, approximately half of all people in the US will experience a diagnosable trauma although more recent studies have it at about 75%. And about 7 or 8 out of every 100 people will have PTSD at some point in their lives. *And that's only diagnosed traumas.* The official "rules" for diagnosing a trauma reaction are pretty limited, which means I consider the number way higher than 8%.

Having suffered abuse as a child is a trauma we all recognize, for example. But having dealt with horrific bullying isn't necessarily a recognized trauma...even though many people have taken their own lives because they were bullied. So no list. Because trauma doesn't operate by checking the right box in the right category. Instead? Please believe me when I say *your experiences and reactions are valid and real and you are worthy of care and the opportunity to heal.*

Because we don't know why some things are worse than others for some people. I know that it is a weird fucking idea, but *everyone is different.* Everyone's *lives, histories, and experiences* are different AND our *genetic predispositions* are different.

And then, get this: We now even know that trauma can actually create genetic changes that can be passed down through generations. If you have a great-grandparent, grandparent, or parent with a serious trauma history, you are wired for a different response than someone who had family members without a lot of life drama. So not only do our genes influence our trauma reactions, our trauma reactions influence our genes.

Seriously, human brain? Could you go fuck yourself on this one?

On a physical level, traumatic response = Amygdala Hijack.

And there are different levels of intensity within that amygdala response. Sometimes we aren't in full-blown trauma mode, but we keep noticing some weird patterns and habits in our thinking and behavior. Maybe you're not in full force freak-the-fuck-out mode but HOLY SHITBALLS, managing yourself is taking away more energy than it should. Ain't nobody got time to spend on the concentrated effort of keeping their shit together for months and years on end.

Short version? We all have our fragile places and we are all susceptible. But for some reason, sometimes we hang in there and sometimes we lose our shit. What's up with that?

HOW OUR BRAINS HANDLE TRAUMA

You know the biggest things that happen to us? The things that we think are the most horrific? These terrible events may not always cause a long-term traumatic response.

About two-thirds of the time, when we experience a trauma, our brains actually don't go into asshole mode. That means that *most of the time* we are eventually able to find a way to make sense of the trauma and recover from it without having enormous long-term consequences. This doesn't mean you didn't deal with something epically craptastic. It just means you were able to find your way through the experience without a long term amygdala hijack.

In a perfect world, bad shit wouldn't happen. Heh, yeah. Good luck to all of us on that one. Second-best scenario is that when bad shit happens, we duck and cover then come out unscathed. And honestly, we do most of the time. Look back on all the fucked up things that you had to handle in your life that didn't create epic crazy-brain in the long term. Not that it was an immediate and flawless recovery, though, right?

Most of the time, **it takes about three months to reestablish equilibrium after a trauma**. That is, after about 90 days, our emotional sensors are no longer operating at hyper warp speed mode, and return to normal.

Using the word *normal* is total bullshit, of course. Of course, it's not really normal, no matter how well you recover. Traumas change us forever. So this so-called normal is more of a *new normal*, in that regard. We find a way to live and cope with the situation that happened, the loss of what the world had been, and an acceptance of what it is now. We still experience feelings surrounding whatever happened—feelings that may never completely go away. But our amygdala isn't super haywire over the situation after a few months. Hijack mode, deactivated.

But approximately a third of the time, after a trauma, we don't recover to a new normal. We have a trauma response instead. And we develop PTSD—Post-Traumatic Stress Disorder.

What is PTSD? The Oxford dictionary defines post-traumatic stress disorder as:

"A condition of persistent mental and emotional stress occurring as a result of injury or severe psychological shock, typically involving disturbance of sleep and constant vivid recall of the experience, with dulled responses to others and to the outside world."

Good definition. Fancy one. But the unfancy version? **PTSD is failure to recover from a traumatic event.** And PTSD is a fucking DEMON.

The National Center for PTSD (VA.gov) has collected research in this regard. What makes you more likely to experience PTSD? A lot of the indicators they found make a ton of sense:

- Being directly exposed as a victim or an in-person witness
- Experiencing something that was very severe, or the person was hurt badly as a result of the incident
- Traumas that were long-lasting
- Believing you were in danger or someone you loved was and feeling helpless to protect them or yourself
- Having had a severe physical or emotional response during the traumatic situation

Our backgrounds can make us more susceptible to a trauma response, as well:

- Having had other traumas at a young age
- Having other mental health problems or having family members with mental health problems.
- Having little support from family or friends, either by not having many individuals or being surrounded by individuals who don't understand your experience.
- Having recently had stressful life changes, or having recently lost a loved one.
- Being female or in a minority cultural group (because you are statistically more likely to experience a trauma to begin with)
- Already using mind-altering substances like drugs or alcohol
- Being younger
- Having less education
- Coming from a cultural group or family system where you are less likely to talk about problems.

No surprises there, I don't think. But the last item on that list is HUGE. Go read that again. When we talk about things, they get better.

But why? Why some people and not others? What's the brain science behind all of this?

It's not about the nature of the trauma so much. Or the severity of it. Or even totally a function of our wiring and our experiences. Those things have an impact on our ability to heal, for damn sure. But if it was that easy we could create an anticipatory flow chart to help us nail who is going to develop PTSD and who isn't. But we can't, because how we heal is as much about our present and near future as it is our past.

Research shows that when we can't get to a new normal, it's because the brain's ability to process the experience is disrupted during the first thirty days after the trauma happened. This is why PTSD cannot be diagnosed in the first month. We don't know yet if we're going to get our shit back together or not.

Those first thirty days are critical. We need time and space to recover, to process what happened, to find ways to make sense of how we want the world to work and our experience of how life actually unfolds. In this time, we need relational supports. Our brains are hardwired to connect, and we get better in connection to other people.

Not having this time and these connections is a damn likely indicator that we are heading into trauma response territory.

And not having this time, or these people, happens for a lot of really good reasons.

See, generally speaking, traumas are not stand-alone experiences. Trauma is often complex and continuous. For example, people who are in abusive relationships well know that one-time offenses rarely happen. The violence is cyclical and ongoing. If you serve in the military or work in a high risk profession, you experience terrible things regularly and know that they can occur at any minute of any day. Trauma puts us in survival mode for that first thirty days. And traumas may be coming so fast and furious that we don't have a moment to stop and breathe. So our brains shut down the trauma-processing experience so we can continue to survive.

The brain is actually being a protective motherfucker when it says "We are still in the foxhole and can't deal with this shit right now!"

Sometimes it isn't a matter of continued trauma, but the demands of our everyday lives that cause this shutdown. Sometimes we don't have the time and space to heal from our grief experience. Because we have to keep getting up in the morning, getting to work, feeding the dog, finding our kid's missing left shoe. There is only so much work our overtaxed brain can handle. Taking care of OURSELVES often becomes a luxury we can't afford, rather than a necessity we can't ignore.

And sometimes our brains just have no mechanism to make sense of the trauma. No matter how much time and space we give ourselves for healing, we can't find a place for the traumatic experience that gives it the meaning we need to move on. That's the storytelling brain again, stuck in telling the same story that just doesn't work.

Whatever the reason, the brain can shut down the healing process at a moment's notice and our "new normal" becomes a trauma-informed experience rather than a healing one. We start avoiding any reminders of our trauma because compartmentalizing is the only way we feel safe.

And human beings are some seriously adaptive motherfuckers. Avoidance techniques can work really well for a really long time.

WHAT TRAUMA LOOKS LIKE ON AN ORDINARY DAY

How do you know you're dealing with trauma?

Once you start operating from a trauma-informed experience (whether full blown PTSD or not), you can see signs of the following in your life as the brain's way of managing your trauma with adaptive strategies. Which is just a grad school word way of saying we create great ways to avoid our trauma responses so we don't have to deal with them. But it's a foundation that was built on unsteady ground. Cracks start to develop.

- **Arousal** – The amygdala is always wearing its crazy pants and you find yourself freaked out when you shouldn't be or don't want to be. You may or may not know why. But your brain may process something it considers a threat that you aren't even cognizant of and all of a sudden you are falling apart in the middle of the grocery store.
- **Avoidance** – You find yourself avoiding things that trigger arousal. Grocery store was bad? I can order my groceries online. Really don't need to leave the house for groceries, right?
- **Intrusion** – Thoughts, images, memories related to the trauma experience start shoving their way up. The things that your brain was protecting you from don't actually go away. And they start bubbling to the surface without your consent or willingness. This isn't the same as rumination, where you worry over a bad memory intentionally, but when stuff shows up when least expected. And you can't manage everything that is bubbling up.
- **Negative Thoughts and Feelings** – With all this other stuff going on is it any wonder that you never just feel good? Or even just OK?

These are the essential four horsemen of the PTSD apocalypse. It's how we diagnose full-blown PTSD. When they're present, it means that at some level you are reliving your trauma in your head at any given moment.

But not everyone having a trauma response has full-blown PTSD. A PTSD diagnosis is a checklist, in the end. Someone who is evaluating you for this diagnosis will be looking to see if you have a given number of these symptoms or more. So some people meet some of the criteria for PTSD, but not enough to warrant a diagnosis.

But not meeting criteria for PTSD does not put you in the all-clear or make you magically feel any better, right? You are clearly not OK now and there is a pretty damn good chance that it is gonna get worse.

The VA figured this out when studying 9/11 first responders. Of the people who had some symptoms of a trauma response but not full blown PTSD, 20% showed a symptom increase that qualified them for a PTSD diagnosis two years later when they were reassessed. *Go fucking figure* that if you keep reliving your trauma, those connections keep reinforcing in your brain.

Thoughts, feelings, and behaviors that are driven by our trauma response can be really difficult things to understand. Not just for the people around us, but even for ourselves. Have you ever had a moment like that? When you were thinking "What the actual FUCK, brain?" We feel clueless and the people who love us feel helpless.

But let's give our dick-for-skittles brain a break here. It's the brain trying to make sense of shit. Shit that may not actually make sense in reality. So it goes all over-reactive in how it demands you respond to certain events. It reminds you of your stories. And those certain memories trigger negative emotions. And the brain reacts in a protective way without you even realizing what's going on.

Ok, then. What kinds of symptoms do we need to watch out for? Good question, smart cookie! The list is a pretty long one.

Reliving the Trauma Symptoms:

- Feeling like you are reliving the trauma even though it's behind you and you are physically safe.
- Dreaming like you are back in the traumatic event (or maybe a similar event).
- Having a huge emotional response when something or someone reminds you about the trauma. Like freaking the fuck out, even though you are currently safe and/or lots of physical symptoms (sweating, heart racing, sweating, fainting, breathing problems, headaches, etc.)

Avoiding the Memories of the Trauma Symptoms:

- Doing things to distract away from thoughts or feelings about the trauma, and/or avoiding talking about it when it comes up.
- Avoiding things associated with the trauma like people, places, and activities. And a lot of times these areas of avoidance get

bigger and bigger. Like avoiding a certain street that an accident happened on. Then the whole neighborhood, then driving in a car at all.

- Needing to feel in control in all circumstances, like sitting in places that feel safest in public places, not having close physical proximity with other people, avoiding crowds. (If you work in a field where safety training is a big thing, this may be automatic and not necessarily mean PTSD.)

- Having a hard time remembering important aspects of the trauma (blocking shit out).

- Feeling totally numbed out or detached from everything or just about everything.

- Not being interested in regular activities and fun stuff. Not being able to enjoy shit, even if it should be enjoyable shit.

- Not being connected to your feelings and moods in general. Feeling just…blank.

- Not seeing a future for yourself, like just more of the same versus things getting better.

Other Medical or Emotional Symptoms:

- Stomach upset, trouble eating, only craving foods that are sugary (therefore more comforting to a stressed out body)

- Trouble falling asleep or staying asleep. Or sleeping a lot but for shit. Either way, feeling fucking exhausted all the time.

- Not having enough fucks in your pocket to take care of yourself in important ways (exercising, eating healthy foods, getting regular health care, safer sex with chosen partners).

- Soothing symptoms away with substances (e.g., drugs, alcohol, nicotine use, food) or behaviors (e.g., gambling, shopping, or dumb endorphin-producing shit like playing chicken with trains).
- Getting sick more frequently, or noticing that chronic physical health issues are getting worse.
- Anxiety, depression, guilt, edginess, irritability and/or anger. (A HUGE number of mental health diagnoses are really just a trauma response that is not being properly treated, sadly.)

Is it any wonder that we get all confused about what is a trauma response versus some other diagnosis? So the easy diagnosis is PTSD. But trauma responses, like I mentioned above, can wear a Halloween mask of other stuff. Depression and anxiety are two big ones. Sometimes trauma responses can even hide themselves as bipolar disorder and schizophrenia. I have worked with more than one person that had a label of a thought disorder like schizophrenia, but when we started discussing the content of their "voices" we realized they were trauma flashbacks. Other ways that trauma responses disguise themselves can be ADHD, anger and irritability, attachment and relationship issues, and a twisted sense of right and wrong.

There is nothing wrong with any of these other diagnoses in and of themselves. Diagnoses can be necessary to get insurance to pay for services. They also serve as a tool among clinicians as a shorthand that is only meant to mean "these symptoms present." And these diagnoses can absolutely exist on their own, without a trauma trigger. But the problem with getting real help is when trauma IS the root cause.

And that is how we set ourselves up for failure. Trauma-related diagnoses are actually more successfully treated than many other mental health issues, *if we understand what the symptoms are a response to and handle them in that context.*

Brain unfuckening is a completely possible thing.

OK. SO IT'S NOT REALLY A TRAUMA. BUT I STILL HAVE A FUCKED BRAIN. WHAT'S UP WITH THAT?

Ok, so you picked up this book because you figured you have some unfuckening to do. But the trauma stuff doesn't really ring a bell for you. That's not your thing. But you don't like some of the stuff going on in your head, and want to do something about it.

Maybe you have a habit of reacting that's less intense than a trauma response, but works essentially the same way. Even if your amygdala isn't in terrorist hijack mode, your memories and emotions are still wired together, right? Your amygdala has it's groove going in a bad habit that is making life harder for you in dumb ass ways.

What is a habit? *A settled or regular tendency or practice, especially one that is hard to give up.* We did something and it worked. We continued to do it and it continued to work. At some point maybe it stopped working as well, if at all, but asshole brain is still grooving along with the story that it works, because it hasn't figured out a better option. So it's still going to trigger an amygdala response, tying memory to emotion. It may not be a hugely overactive trauma-informed response, but it is there nonetheless.

This is why addictions are so hard to treat. Learning to STOP doing something is really hard, once we have wired a particular response. Hence the "Addictions" chapter of this book. Even if you are all, *"Yeah, not a heroin addict, doesn't apply,"* consider reading it anyway. Pretty much great info for everybody.

And yes, behaviors and thinking patterns can· TOTALLY have addictive qualities.

For example, maybe you grew up in a house where no one talked about their feelings. It wasn't encouraged and everyone else became uncomfortable if you tried. You learned pretty quickly that talking about your feelings was clearly against the rules. You weren't abused, you weren't traumatized. But, at the dinner table, if you said, *"My best friend and I had a fight today and I'm really sad and angry,"* it would elicit a response of *"That happens sometimes, dear, please pass the potatoes."*

So if you tried talking about your feelings and were continuously shut down, you probably wired a connection in your brain that having these discussions made other people uncomfortable. This maybe made you feel anxious, or guilty, or frustrated.

Cue twenty years in the future. Your Boo wants you to talk about your feelings. You go into this weird-ass emotional fog whenever you try. Anxious, guilty, frustrated. Boo is all "WTH?" and you have no idea.

The good news is that this book will work for you, too. And it will work faster, because the story doesn't have the far deeper groove that a trauma creates. Your work will be more about pattern recognition and clarity rather than a deeper rewiring response. You'll rock that shit out in no time.

WHAT IF I LOVE SOMEONE WITH A SERIOUS TRAUMA HISTORY?

This is seriously tough, isn't it? You have someone that you care about so much that is really struggling with their trauma recovery. You want to HELP. And feeling unable to do so is the worst feeling in the world. You're at risk of serious burnout and secondary traumatization. Because yeah, watching someone live out their trauma can be a traumatic experience in and of itself.

Two things to remember, here:

- This is not your battle.
- …but people do get better in supportive relationships.

This is not your battle. You don't get to design the parameters, you don't get to determine what makes something better, what makes something worse. No matter how well you know someone, you don't know their inner processes. *They* may not even know their inner processes. If you know someone well, you may know a lot. But you aren't the one operating that life.

Telling someone what they should be doing, feeling, or thinking, won't help. Even if you are right. Even if they do what you say…you have just taken away their power to do the work they need to do to take charge of their life. There are limits to how much better they can really be if they are continually rescued by you.

...but people do get better in supportive relationships. The best thing to do is to ask your loved one how to best support them when they are struggling. This is the type of action plan you can create with a therapist (if either or both of you are seeing one) or ask them in a private conversation.

Ask them. Ask if they want help grounding when they are triggered, if they need time alone, a hot bath, a mug of tea. Ask what you can do and do those things, if they are healthy things to provide.

It may be helpful for them to have a formal safety plan for themselves, with what your specific role will be. This will help boundary your role, and keep you from setting up scenarios when you rescue or enable dangerous and/or self-sabotaging behavior.

You may need to set hard limits. You may need to protect yourself. This isn't just for your well-being, but will help you model the importance of doing so to your loved one.

Love the entirety of them. Remind them that their trauma doesn't define them. Allow them consequences of their behavior and celebrate the successes of newer, healthier ways of being. Be the relationship that helps the healing journey.

TAKE ACTION: NAME THAT BASTARD

Give your negative reactions an actual persona to inhabit. Name it after a heinous ex, a shitty grade school teacher, or Kim Jong-un. Create a whole character for that fucker.

Emotions feel so huge and so nebulous that transforming them into an actual, defined entity that you can battle *really helps*. Then you can have convos with *Donald Trump's Epic Hair Swirl* (or whomever, but personally I think all things negative should be named after that hair) whenever it comes calling.

Now you can focus on that entity the way you would on an actual person that was threatening you in a real-world situation. You can negotiate, you can yell back, you can lock it in a box. It's now at a manageable size of your choosing, with the appropriate amount of ridiculousness in its presentation that you can laugh at it while you kick its ass.

UNFUCK YOUR BRAIN

If we called the first two chapters of this book "This Is Your Brain," the rest of this book would be called "This Is Your Brain on Therapy."

I've worked with children, youth, and adults in recovery from trauma throughout my career. I've found that the following analogy works well for most everyone. Kids like the grossness of it, adults like the symbolic understanding that they get.

Trauma is like a wound that has crusted over the top but hasn't fully healed. It looks closed over, but the infection is still burrowed in under the skin. It festers even when we don't realize it is there, or when we find ways to ignore it. But what happens if we don't clean out that wound?

Kids like this part.

"It gushes out EVERYWHERE! Blood and pus and it HURTS and it's SUPER GROSS!"

Totally.

We have to clean it out for it to heal.

But what about the scar it leaves behind?

Adults like this part.

Scars are badges. They are a reminder that we healed.

We create new ways to feel safe that don't cause us more harm in the long run. We process our experiences with people who are safe and trustworthy and care about us. We retrain our brains to THINK rather than REACT. Those wounds? *We treat them.*

THE FANCY SCIENCE OF UNFUCKING

Because our emotions are tied so closely in the brain to our memory, it makes sense that memories of past events coupled with current experiences can elicit a really strong response.

But our brains aren't actually wired to hold on to certain emotions for long periods of time. Emotions are designed as part of our information feedback circuit.

WE LIKE THAT! MORE OF THAT!

~or~

THAT SUCKS! MAKE IT STOP!

Our emotions influence our thoughts and behaviors. They are meant to be a physiological signal to the rest of the brain. Once they have done their jobs, they are then meant to dissipate.

Do you know how long an emotion is actually meant to last?

90 seconds. Seriously, just one and a half minutes for an emotion to run its course.

But you are calling "bullshit" right now, I know. Because if that were really the case, why do our emotions last hours, days, or years? 90 seconds? Not so much.

Emotions last longer than 90 seconds because we continue to fuel them with our thoughts. We do this by telling ourselves the same stories about the triggering situation over and over. This is when they stop being emotions and start becoming moods.

We also continue to fuel them with our behaviors. My favorite definition of crazy is *doing the same thing over and over and expecting different results*. So when we are reactive instead of proactive, we keep reinforcing the pattern.

Say you got in a terrible car accident driving down First Street. It makes total sense that driving down First Street would send your brain into a shit-fit panic. So you avoid First Street. Eventually avoiding First Street is your *modus operandi* to the point that anything that involves being in the vicinity of First Street doesn't happen. You don't WANT to have a meltdown over the thought of driving down First Street. You want your life back, FFS! But as long as you continue to avoid driving down First Street, you are deepening the groove of that behavior and the feelings of panic that you associate with remembering the accident.

Thinking about the accident becomes something we can't control. Rumination is a form of unwelcome, obsessive attention to our own thought patterns. It's a stuck point. An error in the coding. We ruminate about the accident to the point of thinking we are losing our minds, because it feels like the rumination has taken control.

Basically, we continue to feed that particular emotional response (*anxiety, fear*) and those particular thoughts (*accidents happen on First Street*) by continuing with the same adaptive behavior we originally used to keep ourselves safe (*don't drive down First Street, bad things happen there!*). So we keep the feedback circuit in a perpetual cycle.

Ok, yeah, maybe. But what about all those non-rumination memories? The feelings we will go to the end of the earth to avoid. Instead, maybe you refuse to give ANY attention at all to the idea of driving down First Street.

Ruminate? Not fucking LIKELY.

Fucking brain wiring again. Avoiding a certain emotion makes you hold on to it just as much as ruminating over it does. Remember the infection analogy? It's just festering in there.

Both ruminating and avoiding work exactly the same way...a Mobius strip of *nothing really ever changes and we aren't going to get anywhere*. Rumination is a way of insisting on making sense of an experience, but doing it in a nonsensical way. And avoiding is just refusing to acknowledge it at all, at a conscious level. Rumination and avoidance are ways of trying to control our experience, rather than taking it as the information that it is meant to be and finding ways to process through our responses.

When we hit upon a situation where control is taken away from us, even the memory of that event is SERIOUSLY the most uncomfortable situation in the history of EVER. It's a reminder that we have far less control over the external world than we would like to have. And that is deeply scary shit. Both rumination and avoidance are ways our brain reacts in an attempt to get control back. If I fixate on it, I can figure out a way to keep it from happening again. If I avoid it, I can erase it from existence in the past, present, and future. It feels way safer than remembering something, recognizing it for the event that it was, and then letting it go.

To get to a place where we just feel what we feel? To sit with it for that 90 seconds? To remember that it's just information from our body, part of our feedback circuit? That it doesn't define us? Change anything about the essence of who we are? That it may not even be ACCURATE information about the situation? REALLY FUCKING HARD.

Being triggered means being on shaky ground. We just want the earth to stop moving. We want a sense of control back. If we get a sense that what we thought was solid beneath us was never really solid at all, that means we have to live with constant ambiguity. And ambiguity is completely counterintuitive to the things our brain is trying to do and continuing to tell us in order to help us stay safe. Ambiguity pushes the button: Threat Alert Level Red.

Remember all that fancy brain stuff from the first chapter? Because our brains are hardwired to keep us alive, the instinctual part of our brain takes over when we feel threatened. But unlike the other species we share this planet with, when the threat is over, we aren't good at discharging that threat feeling, getting all those hormones and neurotransmitters out of our system, and going back to our everyday lives.

And the prefrontal cortex cannot *control* our instinctual responses; it can only *elaborate* on them. It can offer different information and different ways of responding. It can test new scenarios. The PFC provides feedback. It can negotiate. But it is NOT in charge in times of high stress. You are not crazy for wondering if your thinking brain has been hijacked by your animal brain. You feel that way BECAUSE IT HAS.

And quite frankly, your animal brain is irritated as fuck at all your epic ingratitude at how hard it is working to keep you alive.

It's not a sign of weakness that it keeps happening. It's a hard-wired survival instinct. You can't forcibly take control back through sheer willpower. Animal brain will win every time and smack you down with a "Hell, naw" when you try.

Healing trauma means working through our shit, rather than trying to overpower it. Instead of full-frontal, *Braveheart*-style attack, we create ways of having new convos that are safe and supported. We don't push out of our comfort zone, we create a larger bubble of comfort zone that helps us roll along until we realize we don't need it anymore.

GETTING UNFUCKED IMMEDIATELY AFTER A TRAUMATIC EVENT

Ok, remember when I was yammering on about all that first thirty days stuff? That this is a really critical time for trauma recovery? Yeah. Because, holy shit. If we are given the time and space to process a huge, horrible thing that happened to us? That makes all the difference in the world.

If you have experience with the military, or with first responders (firefighters, police, EMS) you've heard terms like "after-action report" or "incident debriefing." In a similar way, if you have ever been through the kind of traumatic incident where professionals (police, doctors, etc.) got involved, at some point you had to tell your story.

Talking about what happened is a good first step for most people. The problem with that is if we only get to process at a Dragnet level. You know, "just the facts." It has the potential to separate us even further from the emotional content of our experience by focusing on a recitation of events, rather than a processing out of emotionally-laden memories.

When any event happens, it transforms in that instant from an occurrence to a memory. If we are given the space and support, we are empowered to process that memory on the emotional level it was stored at. *"Just the facts"* is only meant to be the beginning of the healing process, because it is not nearly as helpful as *"all the feels."*

So if someone has handed you this book after a very recent trauma event? They are saying they are there and they want to help.

Or maybe you picked it up yourself because the little voice in the back of your head said you should. Either way? This is the time to take care of yourself, tough stuff. You need the space to heal.

I haven't really found a huge difference between the things that help you heal when a trauma is fresh versus what to do when it is older. But I have found that healing is way easier when we dig into it right away and don't give our brains the opportunity to start mapping out bullshit signals that fuck us up. I also found that if you're able to do the work now, you are far less likely to struggle with chronic mental illness as a result of your trauma, or at least it will be less severe/ more manageable.

And I also know you are worth the time it takes to focus on yourself and your healing. No matter how silly it feels, or how busy you are, or how much everyone around you is dismissive or uncomfortable with the process.

You deserve every opportunity to heal.

UNFUCKING WAY LATER

Then there are us unlucky motherfuckers who didn't get a chance to really unpack our trauma during that 90-day re-stabilization window. That means you have more months, years, or decades of brain fuckery to untangle. This is not a hopeless situation at fucking all. Because if this is you? You are a SURVIVOR. Your brain figured out ways to keep you going when everything around you was crazy. And it WORKED.

The problem is, it isn't working well anymore. Instead of being a solution, it's become a problem. So your brain has to be put back on its leash and retrained.

You need to teach your brain to use the prefrontal cortex to discriminate between real threats and perceived threats again. When the feedback system works the way it's intended to, the amygdala doesn't go nuts and send every message to the brainstem to activate freak-out mode.

A lot of the work I do in my private practice is guiding people through processing their stories while helping them stay grounded in the present. This helps us remember that we are in control of our experience at this point in our lives, even if we weren't in the past. It is amazing to realize you can feel something and not have it overwhelm you. That right there? That is what *taking your power back* really means.

If someone has a partner or supportive friend or family member available, I show them how to help with the process as well. We figure out exactly what their role will be so they have a way of being supportive, rather than freaking out and making the situation worse. (Some of the dumbest stuff is done with the best intentions, right?)

Many people do this work in therapy, but not everyone. Even if you are working with a therapist, a good therapist is going to operate as your sideline coach, giving suggestions and feedback from the outside perspective. If you are working through any of these issues, you are the one doing the hard part, whether your supports are friends, family, or helping professionals, or just your own damn determined will to get better.

Whether you have help or are going it on your own, I've found that knowing why these techniques work make them work that much faster. Knowing how the brain is wired to work helps us feel less frustrated, stupid, and guilty. Because one of the biggest barriers to getting better? Shame. Shame from ourselves and shame from others that we aren't already better. Or that we had an issue to begin with.

And fuck that.

Remember what I said about you being a survivor? If you have crawled through all these years, months, decades of muck, fighting with a haywire brain, YOU DESERVE TO FEEL BETTER. You deserve your life back. You are not fundamentally, unfixably broken.

Let's do the thing.

TAKE ACTION: RIDE THE WAVE

Emotions last 90 seconds. And because you are NOT AT ALL the type of person who reads the text boxes before the actual main text (unlike me), you know that means that emotions are meant to be a signal in the brain that something needs your attention. They are meant to only last long enough to actually get your attention, and they dissipate after you decide on your course of action.

The problem is we tend to do one of two things instead of paying attention. We either perseverate (without action) or go straight-up avoidance mode. Both make brain fuckery worse.

Try setting aside five minutes to sit with the anxiety you're feeling instead of fighting back. All this means is being mindful of your present emotional experience. You can free-write as you are processing. You can practice your breathing. You can do anything other than avoid or distract from the feeling. The point is to retrain yourself that it won't last forever. You may be this feeling's bitch for a few minutes, but this is not a permanent state of being. I swear on my Roomba it won't last forever...and I love my Roomba, it's employee of the month every month!

If you attend to what you are feeling, you get over it way more quickly than if you avoid it. I've noticed I'm bored with myself about 3 minutes into committing to sitting with my feeling for 5. I'm ready to go make a cup of coffee, read a book, find the cookies I hid from myself, or do *anything other than perseverate.*

TAKE ACTION: PUT IT ON ICE

A lot of therapists used to encourage clients to wear a rubber band and snap it on their wrist if they felt an urge to self-harm, or were having spinning thoughts, or considering an impulsive behavior. But, um, snap a rubber band on yourself enough times and you will tear the fuck out of your skin. So we're not doing that anymore.

But the point of the rubber band was legit. We were trying to help people disrupt the current focus of the brain by encouraging it to attend to another pain point. Ice works much better without causing lasting damage. Seriously, try it. Grab an ice cube and squeeze. Your brain is gonna be all "OW! WTF you doing that for??" and it disrupts the signal. If you have an impulse to self-injure to manage anxiety, you can actually place the ice on the part of the body you typically hurt instead of doing the other harm behavior.

The cool thing too, is carrying ice with you isn't obvious. You can bop around in your day, and grab an ice cube out of your cup without people going "What the hell is that about?" I have worked in group programs where everyone carried water, so handing someone a cup full of ice to use if they got triggered didn't make them feel singled out to their peers.

GETTING BETTER: RETRAIN YOUR BRAIN

A FRAMEWORK FOR GETTING BETTER

So this is the general section of the book. Here is how we retrain the brain bullshittery that's going on. Of course, not everyone has the same responses to situations. If they did, fixing shit would be easy and I wouldn't have a job. So topics related to some of the specific things that happen to people are coming up in later chapters. You know...depression, anxiety, anger, addiction, grief responses, and stress. All parts of the human condition at some point in every life.

But first I want to lay a stage-wise model on you...an idea of sequence for how trauma happens that helps us understand how to better fix that shit. I am WAY aware that no one ever fits into a fancy model in which we complete certain steps and then VOILA, ALL BETTER...and let's add some fucking jazz hands to the mix while we're at it.

Life does what it does, and half the time we are just hanging on for dear life. So what other people call stages, I call a framework.

It's good to have an idea of where you are in the process, at any particular moment. So you can focus on what will work best *at that moment*. And if later on today (or next week, or next year) you are five steps forward or two steps back? That's where we go in. No biggie.

Ok, you are squinting at me now with suspicion that we are gonna go all traditional self-help workbook bullshit with a helping of Dr. Phil hollering "How's THAT workin' for ya?" Maybe a tiny bit. But only the shit that works best, nothing extraneous. It's all about the brain science behind it. And F bombs. Because I have a fancy PhD and can say *fuck* as much as I want. So stick with me, and let's figure out what works for you.

Back to frameworks. One of the best frameworks for understanding how the brain heals from trauma comes from Judith Herman's book *Trauma and Recovery*. Her grown-person labels (and my less traditional ones) are listed below:

1. **Safety and Stabilization**
   Holy Shit! That's over, right? I can sit down for a second without someone kicking my ass now? Would that be possible, Universe?

2. **Remembrance and Mourning**
   What the FUCK was that? What happened? Shit ain't supposed to go down like that! That kicked my ass HARD.

3. **Reconnection**
   Ok. So, maybe, just maybe, the whole world isn't complete bullshit and I can still generally be OK again. Not to say that

wasn't some fucked-up shit. But not everything is fucked-up shit and not everyone is a total fucking asshole.

Safety and Stabilization: If trauma means that our sense of safety in the world has been violated, regaining that sense of safety feels almost impossible. That event became a seriously strong memory which continuously triggers our "fight, flight, freeze" response. Safety and stabilization is the process of understanding everything that is going on with your brain and of taking control back over your body when this happens. It's the brain reboot when all this shit gets triggered for you. Herman's book focuses on this stage, and so does mine. Because it's the hardest part to get going…and nothing else happens without it.

Remembrance and Mourning: This is the part we call a trauma narrative. It's the space to be allowed to process your story when you have the skills to do so without being triggered to all shit. It's about owning your story and not letting your story own you. It's about the trauma as you remember it, and the thoughts and feelings that are bundled up with the event memories. If we think of trauma as emotions trapped in the body, this is how we metabolize them out. This can be done in all kinds of safe ways: with a therapist, with an awesome loved one, in a support group, or even by yourself in a journal.

Reconnection: This is a fancy way of saying, "taking your life back." It means finding a way to have the trauma fit into its rightful place within the entirety that is your life, rather than taking over and controlling every aspect of it. It's about finding meaning in your experience. This can be so hard to wrap your head around, I know. This doesn't mean that the situation wasn't horrible and fucked up, but it does mean that you can use it to make yourself stronger, to support others, to not let it own you. It means having positive relationships that are defined by *everything* you are instead of just your trauma. It can also be about reconnecting to your spirituality, if that has been an important part of your identity. It means knowing that no matter what else happens…you have YOU in your corner. A fucking survivor anyone would be lucky to have on their side.

Ok, I admit it's easier to explain than to do, but let's talk about how to get started.

FIRST THINGS FIRST: SAFETY AND STABILIZATION

The following section is full of activities that engage the prefrontal cortex and override the brainstem take-over that puts you into *fight, flight, or freeze* response. Teaching the PFC to focus on something else disrupts the whole asshole brain hostile takeover response.

Bruce Lipton, in his book *The Biology of Belief*, compares trying to stop an amygdala hijack to screaming at a tape player because you don't like the song that's on. It's just playing the tape, yanno? It doesn't have the capacity to realize you want to stop the tape, rewind the tape, or fast forward. It's firing the danger signals and has no more capacity to stop rolling as a tape player has to stop playing a song once the Play button has been pushed. Even if it's Nickelback, FFS.

You CANNOT have a logical conversation directly with the amygdala. ANYTHING you want to do has to be a negotiation with the amygdala by the PFC. Because the amygdala is in protection mode (or terrorist mode, depending on your patience with its bullshit at the moment) and is the one in charge. This is where we re-stabilize ourselves and reestablish our sense of safety. By getting our PFC to sneak in and pause the tape, we can negotiate with the amygdala to chill the fuck out, sit the fuck down, and let the grown-ups get back to work.

Yes, you can actually do something else and think of something else. But you do have to train yourself how.

This trauma response didn't creep up on you overnight, right? You didn't go to bed one night feeling all fine and dandy and wake up the next morning all kinds of hot mess. Your brain created its response network based on the information it was receiving over time, so learning to be un-fucked is also going to take time.

Some days are going to be better than others. You may do awesomely well then get hit like a ton of bricks with all kinds of what-the-SHITSTORM-just-happened???!!!???

Those days are balls, aren't they?

None of that shit makes you a failure, it means you are still growing. I tell my clients "It really is going to be OK in the end. If it's not OK yet, that means we aren't at the end."

And bits of OK now and then give us the breathing room and resting space to store energy for our next battle against that anxiety-trying-to-eat-our-face-off thingy. Ok, that's not the technical term, but it should be.

The biggest component to making this shit work is to practice these techniques when your brain is not in asshole mode rather than trying to learn them when you are already completely stressed. Trying new soothing and coping techniques when you are feeling your best self will help you figure out which ones work for you.

Because as you well know, taking control of your brain back when it's been hijacked is really difficult.

There is an expression: *Amateurs practice until they get it right, experts practice until they can't get it wrong.* I'm not trying to go all inscrutable Zen koan on you here...the idea is that the way to Carnegie Hall is practice, practice, practice. Proving you can do something once is easy, getting so good at it that it becomes your second nature is way harder.

But that's what rewires a trauma reaction. Do it so often it just becomes *what you do*. On Tuesdays we wear pink. And when we are triggered, we use our fucking coping skills.

Trying good coping skills out while you are NOT in freak-out mode will make it easier to access them when you are. Having people around you that feel safe to you and that can help prompt you to use your positive coping skills can be invaluable.

Of course, it probably seems that panic comes on at the worst possible time, when you are on the freeway and alone in the car, for example. So having a set of simple coping skills as well as the more complicated ones is invaluable. It might be a literal talisman (a stone you carry), a mantra you say, or the coping cards from the text box below. Yes, they seem cheesy as fuck. But they WORK so damn well, I gotta throw the idea out there.

TAKE ACTION: CREATE COPING CARDS

The problem with all the coping mechanisms below is that chances are you can't fucking remember them in the heat of the moment, at least at first. So when you find a mantra, a grounding exercise, a fact about anxiety, or another statement or image or action that helps you, put it on an index card. Hole punch your cards, put them on a snap-shut key ring, and you have a set of coping cards you can flip through when panic hits.

It sounds epically nerdy, I know. But I have had so many clients end up loving the shit out of their cards and using them all the time. They're a way to remind the PFC to be in charge of the control stick and ground itself in reality. It's cheese with extra cheese sauce, but that's what works when we are actively rewiring brain bullshittery.

GROUNDING TECHNIQUES

I get asked a lot to teach *just one skill* to people. New counselors, new foster parents, and first responders who aren't counselors but end up helping people manage a mental health crisis all ask, *"What's the one universal thing that anyone can do to help someone having a rough time?"* and the best answer I have is to help people ground themselves back in their bodies and in the present.

When triggered, the brain is reliving a past event instead of responding to the present moment. Grounding activities help you get back in your body and the present moment rather than reliving your memories. Grounding is one of the best ways to manage emotional pain, because it helps you remain in the present and remember that the pain itself is based in memory, and doesn't have the power to hurt you in this moment. I hear all the time from people that they use the shit out of this skill.

Some people don't want to unpack their story and process their trauma. And that's OK. But everyone wants a way to manage all the shit that comes up when they are experiencing a trauma reaction. Grounding helps a lot. Seriously. It's the best way of saying *"Hey, amygdala? Slow your roll, FFS."*

MENTAL GROUNDING

Mental grounding techniques are intended to keep you in the present moment by focusing on your current situation and surroundings. You are gonna use mantras or make lists. And yes, you can say these out loud. To yourself, to someone else. If you're on the city bus and don't want to draw attention, you can go through your list mentally or mutter under your breath. Whatever works. (…and if you put in headphones, people will think you are singing to yourself and not responding to internal stimuli.)

For example, you might describe all the colors in the room, or an object you are holding.

It may be repeating a safe phrase to yourself over and over. One of my favorites that I heard recently was "FUCK YOU, AMYGDALA!" It apparently works beautifully for that individual!

Some people like to play a kind of categories game, where they name all their favorite movies, or books, or something that requires a different kind of concentration.

Some people will go over their schedule, either in their mind or out loud, or the steps needed to complete an activity.

All of these mental grounding activities are a way to remind your brain of where you are in the moment and that you have more control than you realize over what is going on inside you when your panic button has been tripped.

PHYSICAL GROUNDING

As young children, we are in our bodies and in our experiences all the time. It isn't until we get older that we realize our bodies can be in one place while our mind goes somewhere else. This is great when your body is in math class but your brain is on the playground. But it becomes more problematic as we get older. Have you ever found yourself arriving at home without remembering anything about the trip it took to get there? Physical grounding techniques are ways of reminding us that we are in our bodies and that we have ownership of that experience.

Physical grounding can include being mindful of our breathing. Simply notice your breathing, in and out. When you catch yourself wandering, remind yourself to focus back on the breath.

You may try walking and noticing each step you take. If you find that you walk and still ruminate, try carrying a teaspoon of water while you walk, and focus on trying not to spill drops of it.

Touch objects around you.

Sometimes specific sensory objects are especially soothing. These are usually suggested for people who respond differently neurologically (you know, people with autism spectrum-type wiring) but they can help everyone. Things like: A cotton ball with lavender oil on it kept in an airtight container that can be opened and sniffed to trigger a calming response. Something to chew on (gum, beef jerky). Play-doh that can be squished, glitter bottles that can be shook, a talisman in your pocket like a polished stone or something of spiritual significance. A ring that you can spin on your finger.

Jump up and down.

Make sure your feet are touching the floor. Try taking off your shoes and feeling the ground beneath you.

Eat something slowly and be mindful of all the flavors and textures. Grapes or raisins work well for this. Interestingly? People who don't even like raisins (and I raise my hand here) are not bothered by them when using them for this exercise.

If you feel safe to be touched, have someone you trust put their hands on your shoulders and remind you gently to remain in your body.

If touch isn't going to make things worse? Give someone a hug. Go get a massage. Cuddle with your boo. Touching and being touched releases oxytocin. Touch is also good for the heart and the immune system. So get on that.

SOOTHING GROUNDING

Soothing grounding is essentially self-compassion and self-care in a difficult situation.

Think of things that make you feel better. Visualize things you enjoy, such as the beach or a sunset. A sunset on the beach? I'm down with that.

Remember a safe place and picture yourself surrounded by that safety.

Plan an activity or treat you can look forward to in the near future, like a cupcake from your favorite bakery, a hot bath, a movie you've seen 100 times and still adore, a baseball game and a bowl of popcorn, or a hike in your favorite park.

Carry pictures of people and places you care about and focus on these images.

You can play with all of these different forms of grounding, and develop ones that work best for you when you are feeling most distressed. If you are intrigued by the idea of doing more work in this area, you may want to check out some of the recommended reading at the end of this book as well.

But above all else? You totally got this shit. Your brain has done its job in keeping you safe, and now you are ready to take the reins back and move forward in your life. And that's excellent, isn't it?

GETTING HELP WITH GROUNDING

If you have someone who is supporting this work, share this with them and ask them to prompt you through your re-grounding process.

If you are reading this to help someone who is struggling to try new coping techniques, this is something you can offer gently or even model, without saying, "Hey, I'm going to help you with your fucked brain right now." For instance, I might drop some essential oils on the lightbulbs in my office and talk about focusing on the scent. I'm already usually barefoot, so I will talk about how I like to feel my feet directly against the ground. I may gently discuss the colors on the walls, the textures on the blankets in the room, the sensory materials we have for kids that all of us adults love too.

If I notice panic coming up in a friend or family member I know well enough to touch even when they are triggered, I may put my hands on their shoulders and press down very slightly while talking to them about what I notice going on.

Many counselors are now using sensory tools that our occupational therapy cousins have been talking about for decades. Small weighted blankets with just enough size and weight to place across your lap, feet, or around your neck can also be really helpful.

MINDFULNESS MEDITATION

Ok, first of all let's start by getting all definition-y. We tend to use mindfulness and meditation as interchangeable terms. Or in a non-interchangeable but still confusing-as-fuck way. They aren't really meant to be interchangeable, but they aren't really meant to be confusing-as-fuck either.

Meditation is when you intentionally set aside time to do something that's good for you. There are all kinds of meditations (prayer, exercise, art, etc.).

Mindfulness is both a general awareness of the world (noticing your existence and the existence of everything else around you) AND formal meditation practice. It's two things, not one.

So you can meditate without being particularly mindful and you can be mindful without meditating. But meditation and mindfulness overlap when we do **mindfulness meditation**, which means that we are setting aside time for that intentional focus on our awareness of the world…which includes the workings of our own mind.

I've included some of my favorite books on the subject in the recommended reading list. There are people who are way smarter than me about this shit. But here's the basic guideline to get you started.

Sit upright. If you can do this without back support, like on the floor on a cushion then good on you. If you need a straight back chair, do that. If you can't sit at all, that's OK, too. Get yourself in whatever position is most comfortable. The reason sitting is better than laying down is that the point is to fall awake, not fall asleep. But the point is also to not be in screaming fucking pain, so don't stress it.

Soft-focus your eyes so they aren't closed but they are seeing without actually seeing. You know what I mean. Be visually spaced out because what you are really going to be paying attention to is inside you.

And now you are going to breathe in and out. And focus on your breath. If you have never done this before it's going to be weird and hard. But for the record, if you have done this a zillion times chances are still good that it will be weird and hard.

If you catch yourself being distracted, just label it "thinking" and go back to focusing on your breath. Thinking isn't a failure in the least. It's gonna happen. And noticing it and bringing the mind back to the present moment is the point. So it's a total win.

A lot of people feel awful during meditation, thinking they suck at it because they are continuously distracted by chatting thoughts. That's OK. Your brain is desperately seeking to story-tell. All kind of distracting stuff is going to come up. You are going to think about what you need to cook for dinner. Or a conversation you had at work. Or whether or not you should buy new sneakers or go to a movie this weekend.

Because the default network of the brain is storytelling mode, remember? And you aren't distracted by external events, so the default mode has all kinds of stories to tell you. But here is the thing about mindfulness meditation…research shows that it disrupts the storytelling process of the default network. When we used to think the only way to do that was a distraction by outside events and stimulus.

And I'm not even going to pretend that this shit is easy to do when you are spun up. But it's important to at least try. Because part of a panic attack is the stories our brain starts telling us about the attack itself. And it's generally not a pretty story. Because the chemicals released during an anxiety or panic attack are designed to get your breathing ramped up and your heart racing. So your brain is insisting that you are going to have a heart attack or stop breathing. That's not actually going to happen. When you catch that thinking, remind yourself that's a biochemical response, but not reality.

Keep breathing. The continued, conscious effort to breathe and un-tense will slow your heart rate back down and help you get more oxygen flowing. It's a literal chemical counter-balance. Meditation releases every chemical that counteracts brain fuckening: dopamine, serotonin, oxytocin, AND endorphins. And it's cheaper than Crossfit. Six thousand years of Buddhist practice has something going for it, yeah?

Treat your bodily reactions like any other random thought. Itching is common. If you catch yourself itching, label it *thinking* three times before succumbing to the urge to scratch. You may be surprised at how often your brain is creating things for you to focus on. As an early meditator, my nose would start to run. My meditation instructor got wise to my epically awesome self-distraction skill and started keeping tissues by her cushion for me. I wasn't allowed to get up. I used a tissue and went back to my breathing. Of course, if you have real pain, don't ever ignore that. Rearrange yourself for comfort and don't be a hero.

If you have someone helping you through this, they can prompt your mindfulness by saying something like, "Hey, what are you noticing going through your head right now?" or progressive relaxation by saying, "Ok, let's start with your hands. They're really clenched up, can you spread out your fingers instead of balling your hands up?" Sometimes meditation feels more doable if you have someone meditating with you—it helps you feel supported and kept on track.

PRAYER

So we just defined mindfulness meditation, right? Meditation is no more than **listening to.** Meditation is the process of quieting ourselves down enough to hear what's going on inside us. Our minds are brilliant at creating endless amounts of chatter that we often talk back to without listening first. Meditation is the willingness to hear yourself before you speak.

What does prayer have to do with it? You may be rolling your eyes up in your head at me over this one, I know. Prayer? I don't do religious. But what we have, as a culture, agreed to call prayer is just **talking to.** Speaking to ourselves or something bigger than ourselves about our wants, needs, desires, and intentions. Remember the storytelling brain? Prayer is a natural mechanism of the storytelling brain. Talking through our situation in this manner can be far more powerful than talking to a friend, family member, or therapist. It's a grounding experience that helps us be more aware of our thoughts, feelings, and behaviors. This is what is going on. This is what I want. This is the help that I need.

MUSIC

Because who doesn't like music, right? Only the same people who hate the smell of home baked bread and don't understand how adorable fluffy baby sloths are.

Do you know how much of our day we spend listening to music? Like FOUR fucking HOURS. Music is primal. MIT scientists recently figured out ways to prove that we have specific neurons in the brain that pay attention only to music, ignoring all other audial noises. Brains have music rooms. And, just maybe, music existed before speech did. And that's why speech developed at all…to go with our music. And look at how much of our early architecture was designed around our need for music. Across cultures, places of worship were designed around our need to create music in communion.

Music is both primal and communal.

And we all use music in different ways. Some people want music that is soothing when they are distressed. Others want to hear things that are loud and thrashy and match what is going on inside. Still others want things that are upbeat and danceable so they can have their *Ellen* moment.

I grew up listening to old blues albums on vinyl while the other, less weird kids were watching *Sesame Street*. So guess what is most soothing for me? Old blues albums on vinyl. Or when I need a pick-me-up, I like to pull up the music I work out too. It has a cadence that I connect to physical movement. I may use it to dance around to while cleaning the house, or even while driving to prepare myself for the event I'm driving to.

What works for you?

Having music that helps your brain connect to either a relaxed state, or an energized but not panicked state can be really beneficial. Especially now when everyone, including those baby sloths, have smart phones that they can cue up a playlist on. So create a couple of playlists. Think about what your songs are. What's your fight song? Your personal anthem? The songs that reflect your best self? The songs that remind you that life is worth living? Have them ready to cue up when you need them.

SELF-COMPASSION EXERCISES

Self-compassion is the total polar opposite of self-esteem. Self-esteem comes from the outside. Do great on a test? Great for the self-esteem. Fuck it up royally? Self-esteem is shot to shit.

Self-compassion means being as kind to yourself as you would your best friend. It is an intentional honoring of our imperfections as humans. It doesn't mean we let ourselves off the hook for things we fuck up, and it's not an excuse to be a dick. In fact, people who are self-compassionate are also more driven to be better human beings because they think they are worth the effort.

Treat yourself with kindness, understanding, and self-respect. Ask yourself, what would you say if this was happening to your best friend? What would the Buddha say to you right now?

Amazing things have happened when I have taught people the self-compassion skills suggested by Kristen Neff and Christopher Germer (see the recommended reading section for their work). The first time it happened, I was teaching a room full of therapists working on their research PhDs. One of these people also happened to already be an MD.

So, you know. Strong, focused, high achievers like whoa. I asked them to put their hands over their hearts and remind themselves that they experience suffering. That this suffering is part of the human condition. And to give themselves permission to be kind to themselves and forgive themselves their imperfections.

The aforementioned MD/PhD/SuperFancyPants therapist? She did the exercise and tears started to roll down her face. This person, who I looked up to as amazing, had never slowed down long enough to give herself the same level of compassion she showed to the individuals she worked with.

Try it yourself.

> *Put your hand over your heart and voice your experience of suffering. Remind yourself that suffering is part of humaning. Tell yourself that you are allowed kindness and forgiveness, and that starts as an inside job.*

MANTRAS/POSITIVE SELF-TALK STRATEGIES

Does this make you feel like Stuart Smalley? I always felt cheesy when I tried positive self-talk but I also found that it WORKED. Think of it as talking over that bullshit tape the amygdala is playing.

> *Yes, I know you are freaking out right now. It will pass and you will feel better. Keep breathing.*

> *You've got this. It may not feel like you do. But your success rate for getting through serious bullshit is 100%. You aren't about to break your winning streak.*

> *You know what sucks? This right now. You know what helps? This isn't permanent. And you've totally earned a cookie for dealing with this today.*

Your self-talk strategies can be put on your coping cards if you are using them. And this is absolutely something you can ask for help with. Let people know which mantras you are using and have them remind you of them when you are struggling.

EXERCISE

I know, I know. Fuck Crossfit and fuck spinach smoothies. But exercise releases endorphins. Short version of that? Endorphins have mad ninja skills...they block our perception of pain and enhance positive feelings...both of which counterbalance the stress response. Which means those superfit people who say they get a runner's high? Totally aren't lying. Freaks of nature, maybe. But totally telling the truth.

You are totally allowed to choose a form of exercise you can tolerate. I am not a fan of sweating and physical exertion in the name of health. But my doctor keeps telling me that reaching for a cookie does not count as a sit-up, so I gotta do SOMETHING. I do enjoy swimming, walking, and hiking...they are way more relaxing and meditative for me than competitive team sports (but if that's your thing...go on with your weird-ass self!). Even better is when I go hiking with my bestie. We get exercise and get to talk shit about everyone we know in the process.

Find something that doesn't suck. It can be as intense or gentle as you want, but try stuff. Most places will offer a free class or free week so check shit out. I had a client who fell in love with boxing by trying out a free class. It was great exercise AND made her feel more empowered and in control of her experiences.

GET YOURSELF OUTSIDE

Sometimes the doing of anything feels like way more than can be handled. Remaining vertical is difficult enough, there certainly isn't going to be any meditation or exercise or any other woo-woo shit.

If you can't do anything else, try to get yourself out in some sunshine. Even if it's just to sit on a bench while drinking your afternoon coffee or something. Sunlight increases vitamin D production and serotonin. Both of which will give you a little chemical boost without having to pop a pill. It's hard to sit in the sun and feel like ass at the same time. And trust me, I've tried. I usually perk up despite myself.

If you live in a grey and gloomy place, you may want to invest in a personal sunlight lamp that you keep on your workspace. When my brother left Texas to go to school on the East Coast, he found himself battling seasonal affective disorder (SAD). He just wasn't getting enough sunlight to battle low-level blues. The lamp made a huge difference.

WHEN YOU'RE READY: REMEMBRANCE AND MOURNING

Once you have a number of skills down that help you manage the responses that have been managing you, you may be thinking about working through your story.

The good coping skills part is really fucking important. So many people feel forced to talk about what is going on with them without a way to feel safe in the process. It's triggering as hell and ends up retraumatizing them.

So these techniques are things you only do when you are ready, when and if telling your story is something that is going to help you move on, and with someone who can be with you in that experience.

WRITING OR JOURNALING

Writing or journaling exercises, especially when taking the time to be slow and deliberate and put pen to paper, can be a good start for sharing your story. Things may come out that you didn't realize were there, or that you needed to say. Some ideas to get you started may include:

- Use a workbook that includes specific writing prompts related to your situation. For example, many individuals who have dealt with childhood sexual trauma have found the writing exercises in *The Courage To Heal* by Ellen Bass and Laura Davis to be very useful. I have clients that complete the exercises between sessions and we review what they wrote together.

- Write letters to other people. Not letters you will actually send, but what you would want to tell them if you could. This may be the people who hurt you. Or it may be the people who you love but who don't understand what you are struggling with. Figuring out what you want them to know might be a good starting point for understanding your own process. And maybe starting a new conversation with them, if possible.

- Write a letter to your future self. Write about everything you went through to get to the healthiest place you are working toward in your future. List all the things you went through and how you got through them…as if you already have. What you come up with may surprise you.

TELLING YOUR STORY

This simply means talking about your trauma and other things that have impacted your life, as you remember and perceive them. This isn't about literal truth, but the story you have been carrying with you that has affected your wiring for so long.

We talked about the brain being a storytelling brain. Creating a new story means first understanding the one we are now carrying around. Sometimes the story ends up surprising us. We don't even realize all the hateful shit we are telling ourselves until it happens in our out-loud voice.

Preparing people to do this part is a big part of trauma therapy. But many people are able to do it with the help of friends, family, or other loved ones. While group therapy can be really beneficial, this probably won't be the place where you tell all the details of your story, as it can be a triggering experience for other group members. In my years of group work, we would create a title for the event (e.g., "when the rape happened"), when processing issues surrounding the event, but wouldn't discuss details of the event itself during group.

The actual work of sharing the story usually starts with a trained therapist…because we have the skill set to hold space for you and are able to sit with all the strong feelings that are coming up for you without judgment, correction, or our own experiences being triggered.

If you do want to have this conversation with a friend, family, or other loved one instead, keep in mind that the person may be going through their own shit. Hearing your shit may not be something they can handle, and that's totally fair. They may think they can, but then realize they are getting triggered. Before you start, give them permission to stop at any point. Many times people share their stories with a therapist first and then invite the loved one in and share the story again to that person, with the therapist present to help the process.

REFRAMING YOUR STORY

Telling our story in a coherent way can often help us figure out the parts of the story that don't make sense, or to see other perspectives. We may find that there was more going on than is on the tape we have been playing over and over in our heads. It doesn't make horrible experiences less horrible, but it can help us find meaning and work towards forgiveness.

Remember all that brain science stuff about how we have an emotional response and then we create a story to back up that response? One of the best things you can do to challenge that is to *think about how you are thinking.*

Here's the magic. Brains are changing all the time…and we can shape that journey. Yes, trauma changes our genetic structure but we can change it back. Life experiences reshape our DNA moment by moment. The Dr. Faith guide to epigenetics would be a whole other book, but what you need to know is that we are not destined to a prison of our past experiences.

1) Think about the story you tell yourself and others. Review the story that you shared from the exercise above. What aspects might be missing? What else needs to be included?

2) How is this a story of your survival?

3) Who are the other good guys? The caretakers and the helpers? What did they do and how did they do it?

4) What about the things you did that you aren't proud of? In what ways were they the best decision you were able to make for yourself at the time? What did you learn from them that you can use moving forward?

GETTING BACK OUT THERE: RECONNECTION

Reconnection means reconnecting to ourselves and to the world around us. It is how we re-engage, make peace with our brains, and live a full life. This part can be a struggle, because we are so often pushed to do this before we are ready…before we feel safe. And clearly it doesn't work that way. When your "reconnection" is forced by the will of others, it becomes another form of trauma…because your power was taken away from you. Again.

You do this when YOU are ready. And yes, you may need to push yourself a bit. But now you have the grounding and coping skills to remind yourself that you are safe.

You got this.

USE YOUR STORY TO CREATE MEANING

The healthiest people are the ones who find meaning in chaos. The ones who can find the pony in a pile of shit every time.

It doesn't make the awful things that happen any less awful with bullshit like *"Oh, that was God's will, there was a lesson to be learned in that."* Because if God wanted me to learn something, there were far easier ways of making that happen, I'm pretty sure.

But we can learn skills of resilience and strength through the terrible things that happen. They can make us better, stronger, more compassionate, more engaged human beings.

1) **Learn from your past.** Your past is your learning experience, not the well-worn rut your brain keeps trying to live in. What have you learned that you want to carry forward? What have you learned about yourself and your capacity to survive and heal? What can you let go of so you can move on?

2) **Learn from your future.** You know where you want to go, what kind of person you want to be. Ask that person what you need to do now to get there. Ask them to share their secrets of success.

3) **Use both in your present.** Continue being aware of what and how you think. What from your past are you carrying? What from your future? What do you have to offer others as a benefit of what you have gone through? What empathy and support can you share? How can you help others not be alone? How can you advocate for change in your community?

FINDING FORGIVENESS

Forgiveness is serious, deep, and powerful magic. So many people think that forgiveness means forgiving those who have hurt them. And there is truth to that. But more so, I have found people really are working to forgive THEMSELVES. The person they are angriest at and ashamed of is THEMSELVES. And they have been carrying the weight of that around for years.

Reminding yourself that you were doing the best you could with the information and skills you had at the time is hugely important. And remembering that the people who have hurt us are also broken and fucked up is almost as important.

Thich Nhat Hanh is a well-known Vietnamese Zen monk and teacher. He is the man Martin Luther King Jr. called "an apostle of peace and nonviolence" when nominating him for the Nobel Peace Prize.

He is also a man who had a very abusive father growing up. He talks about picturing his father as a three-year-old boy, before the world reshaped him into the angry man he became. And he states that he pictures himself as a three-year-old boy, standing in front of his father. His three-year-old self smiles at his three-year-old father, who then smiles back.

He doesn't call it a forgiveness practice, but it absolutely is. Remember that self-compassion stuff from earlier in the book? Compassion is integral to forgiveness. First ourselves, then others.

BUILDING RELATIONSHIPS WITH SAFE BOUNDARIES

Nobody sets out to have shitty relationships. But we do have a habit of picking people to be with who allow us to keep playing the same tapes over and over. When you have ownership of your story, you can figure out how to stop the tape and get back in charge of your brain, and you will be amazed at the amount of bullshit you were putting up with around you.

You will be able to articulate clear boundaries for yourself and unfuck your relationships in the process. You may start letting people out of your life, when you realize they can't deal with your new backbone. That can be a really difficult thing to process. Make sure you have support of healthier people around you that support your boundary work while you make this transition.

If your boundaries have been violated in the past, you may not know how to create boundaries that aren't too rigid or too permeable. Start by asking yourself the following questions:

1) Is this a person who challenges me to be my best self or are they here because I prefer them to being alone?

2) Is being alone the same thing as being lonely? If not, how do I tell the difference and how do I manage them as different situations?

3) Have I (or am I) communicating my boundaries effectively or am I expecting other people to figure out what I want?

4) What are my boundaries? What are deal breakers? What is possibly negotiable? What is not an issue?

5) Have these boundaries changed over time? Do I see them maybe changing in the future?

GETTING (PROFESSIONAL) HELP: TREATMENT OPTIONS

There are lots of ways to kick your brain's ass back into shape. And a lot of them will be things you do on your own.

But sometimes on your own isn't enough. If you aren't getting better, or not getting better at the rate you would like to see, it might be useful to get help with someone who has the skills, resources, training, and perspective on your situation that you don't have.

My intent here is to help you consider different ways you can best bring yourselves back to wellness. Many of the things I have found to help are things that have not been common in Western medicine practice. I've noticed that this is seriously changing, though. And changing fast.

About ten years ago I had a client discharge from the local state hospital with melatonin instead of Ambien and I think I actually squealed out loud, I was so excited. Ambien is a pretty strong sedative, typically prescribed for insomnia. You've probably heard stories of the crazy shit people have done sleepwalking on Ambien.

Melatonin on the other hand is a supplement you can purchase over the counter. It's a hormone that we naturally produce that helps us tune into our sleep cycle. Many of the people who use it have found that it not only helps them fall asleep, it helps them stay asleep—without the prescription requirement, side effects, and price tag of Ambien. That particular change was the first step I saw on a shifting focus in medicine. I am seeing more and more Western practitioners (like myself) incorporating complementary, holistic treatment or referring our patients out for it.

Yes, I am one of those people who loves woo-woo. But I believe in *evidence based woo-woo*. Anything I have ever suggested has mad research behind it that I can show to my clients and the other people involved in their care. I've had amazing convos with medical doctors in my community when I've touched base about adding complementary therapies and sharing the research I've collected.

You'll read about a lot of kinds of *complementary medicine* below. It is called that for a reason. It is intended to augment, not necessarily replace. I was trained in (and am licensed in) traditional talk therapy. And I would NEVER suggest dumping the prescription medications that have helped people stay alive.

But I also believe in moderation…including in moderation itself! So let's review the treatment options out there that may be of benefit to this brain business that is going on with you.

TRADITIONAL TALK THERAPY

So, yeah. This is my jam. I'm a licensed professional counselor. I'm a talk therapist through and through. Talk therapy has a great capacity to heal, in support of other treatments or sometimes alone. A good therapist has the benefit of their training and a perspective on your life that you don't have because they aren't living the experiences you are living, at least at this time. They can provide insight, coaching, and interventions to help on your getting-bettering journey.

If you are looking for a therapist, you want to work with someone that is *licensed*. Life coaches and other certified professionals and the like can do amazing work, but likely don't have the training and resources to help you through the more intense emotional work that a therapist does. In fact I work with a number of people with these types of certifications who partner with me to make sure someone is available if the work they do with a client triggers a trauma response that they can't handle.

If you are working through trauma, look for a therapist who has had trauma training and find out which kind of training and what certifications they have. All this should be on their website, and don't be shy in asking if it isn't!

If you know you prefer a certain style of therapy, like cognitive behavioral therapy for example, look for that information. If a certain spiritual background is important to you, seek that out as well!

ALLOPATHIC MEDS

Allopathic just means mainstream treatment. Western medicine. The shit we already know about. The prescription stuff. Nothing wrong with allopathic treatment, medication saves lives. If I break my arm, I don't want someone to rub herbs on it, I want it reset and cast.

The problem? As a society, we are moving more and more towards medication as the first (and only) line of defense for managing mental illness, rather than focusing on the root causes. Anxious and depressed? We have medications for that. And rather than using them to help alleviate symptoms while doing other work on the root causes, it becomes a routine of constant medication adjustment with little other support.

This leads to over-medication, tons of side effects, and then more medications to manage the side effects. We are seeing more and more stories of people medicated to the point of toxicity.

And medications don't really work as well as their manufacturers spend advertising billions for us to believe. Most people end up not taking them after a while for just that reason. And the World Health Organization confirmed a long term study which showed that in third world countries where antipsychotic medications are not even available, recovery rates were actually HIGHER. Because if the medications weren't available, they couldn't be the focus of treatment. So the causes were treated. A sense of meaning and community was provided instead. And people got better.

Allopathic medicine doesn't have to be—and often shouldn't be—the endgame of your treatment. But in some cases, it helps the getting-better part happen faster. My friend Aaron is an MD (yes, a REAL doctor who can prescribe meds, unlike me who just talks about shit) uses this analogy:

> Imagine you are in a boat in the middle of the ocean and there is a leak in the hull. You might be able to drop a pump down in the bilge and keep enough water out to make it to shore. You might be able to reach down under the water and patch the hole. But, it would probably work a lot better if you used the pump to lower the water level so you can get at the hole better. The medicine is the pump that will keep you afloat while you and the therapist patch the hole together.

Yeah, yeah. Meds help sometimes. But how? If we know that a trauma reaction changes brain chemistry, what are meds doing to help fix it? To unrepentantly jack another Dr. Aaron analogy?

> Imagine you are an Air Force base. Everything is fine then all of a sudden all the lights go out and the radar goes dead. You aren't going to assume that just because a second ago everything was fine it still is. You are going to assume an attack. When you have a mood disorder your radar has lost communications to the rest of the base, so it assumes an attack, all the time. We are going to

reconnect communications so your threat detector,
which we assume is doing its job, is talking with the
threat response unit again.

Prozac was introduced in 1987, 30 years before the publication of this book. It was the first of many antidepressants to hit the market in the following years. However, suicide rates have kept climbing in the US. And this is exactly why the Dr. Aaron analogies are so brilliant. Medication as tool. Medication as something potentially life-saving. NOT medication as singular cure-all. And it should never be a mechanism for controlling *people* instead of *symptoms*, which is happening more and more. Certain populations, like prison systems and foster care systems receive psych meds at way higher rates than their peers. Which is way too fucking Orwellian for my perspective on healing.

There is a growing trend of distrusting allopathic psych meds. But one side-effect of this trend is that it is actually INCREASING the stigma and shame about mental illness.

The more we can do to encourage the body's own ability to adapt and heal, the better. Medications can be an integral part of that journey, although are rarely the only tools we use. Educating yourself and advocating for yourself about prescription medications will greatly increase the likelihood that they are used properly with you. There are good quality informational portals like the Mayo Clinic, WebMD, and FamilyDoctor that can help you read more about the different types of medications for mental health issues so you can make a more informed decision about what you put in your body.

NATUROPATHIC MEDS

I know, I know: "Here, chew this bark" seems pretty sketch.

Part of the reason that dietary supplements get a bad rap is because many of the ones on the market are complete crap. Just in 2015 the New York Attorney General tested a bunch of supplements and sent a multitude of cease and desist letters to herbal supplement companies based on the fact that much of what they tested had no active ingredient. And the University of Guelph in Canada studied a bunch of supplements and found many unlisted ingredients within them, many that could encourage an allergic response in someone taking them. Or they are synthetic versions of the product rather than the actual extracted herb or whole food. And synthetics are generally going to have more side effects because the human body struggles to recognize them as nutrients.

So yes, the research about the efficacy of certain herbs and food supports are legit. And then we feel stupid and/or ripped off when they don't work on us. I had that experience with a cheap Kava I tried years ago. It made me seriously irritable and not-just-a-little batshit. I was afraid to try Kava again until I learned more about finding and using quality products. I was great about educating myself on prescription meds, but it somehow never occurred to me that I should treat supplements just as seriously!

Now I'm a huge fan of using whole food and herbal supplements in support of or instead of prescription medications. It is something worth talking about with your healthcare provider. Lots of Western medicine docs are getting on board, and there are lots of legit holistic practitioners out there, as well.

When it comes to managing stress, anxiety, depression, and other trauma related symptoms, there are certain formulas that have been used with efficacy for centuries. Kava, as mentioned above, is a good example. As is St John's Wort…and perhaps others you have seen on the news. My recommendations are usually dependent on the specifics of my client's presentation and trauma reactions, but that's an entirely different book. And yes, one I promise I'm writing!

It is SERIOUSLY worth seeing an herbalist, Chinese medicine practitioner, or a clinical nutrition practitioner before you start buying out your local health food store. You don't have to purchase fancy and expensive programs or cleanses to benefit from naturopathic care.

OTHER COMPLEMENTARY THERAPIES

Complementary therapies are not designed to diagnose or treat conditions. They ARE designed to support the body's natural ability to heal. I love the approach of giving my body and mind what it needs to care for itself whenever possible. A lot of treatments have tons of support behind their efficacy. And many of them can be used either alone or with Western practices (like traditional talk therapy or allopathic meds). Some of the most common, with the most research behind them include:

ACUPRESSURE / ACUPUNCTURE

Acupressure and acupuncture use the same principles, but acupuncture involves using the actual needles in the skin while acupressure involves the tapping of certain points instead of breaking the skin.

However, whether tapping or using needles, it works by stimulating certain points on the body to promote healing and/or reduce pain. What is really interesting is that as we learn more about the vagus nerve system, we are seeing lots of commonality in nerve mapping and 5000-year-old acupuncture charts. We know that trauma reactions are a whole body response when we look at the bullshit the limbic system tries to do to us, right? A lot of this response is communicated in the body through the vagus nerve I just mentioned. So there is something to all that weird fucking needle stuff, after all!

If you are interested in a combo deal of acupressure with talk therapy, there are forms of acupressure that some therapists use...most frequently Emotional Freedom Technique (EFT), which combines acupressure and self-talk strategies. The EFT is something you do yourself with guidance from the practitioner, using the same main activation points an acupuncturist uses (bonus if people touching you squicks you out). The self-talk helps you reframe the stories your brain has been telling you while creating new ones in the process. There are a ton of free videos that walk you through the basic process, though a therapist will help you modify the scripts to work through your specific situation.

MASSAGE

Everyone knows what massage is, I don't have to explain it. But people are surprised when I suggest it as healing for emotional issues, not just physical pain. First of all, physical pain can absolutely be a symptom of depression. But even if that isn't going on, massage can be a safe way for people to learn to relax and feel comfortable in their skin. Massage functions as a reset of the nervous system. So many times after a trauma, we feel disconnected from our bodies. I also realize massage can be very triggering for certain types of trauma. Definitely don't force yourself out of your comfort zone. Some people are way more comfortable with a pedicure and a foot massage than with a full body massage. Some people prefer a hot bath or hot tub soak rather than having someone's hands on their skin. Anything that feels safe for you while helping you reconnect with your physical body can really help you unfuck way faster.

CHIROPRACTIC TREATMENT

What? Chiropractic care for mental health issues? Isn't that for bad backs? Beyond again, the fact that depression can manifest as physical pain, chiropracty is a holistic form of treatment that operates from the idea that adjustments can facilitate nervous system support. Pain and nervous system support? Totally huge parts of a trauma reaction for many people. And sometimes these physical symptoms are far worse than the emotional ones.

Many chiropractors (as well as massage therapists and acupuncturists) also build nutritional assistance into their work, as well.

ENERGY HEALING (REFLEXOLOGY, REIKI)

Energy healing is one of those things that seemed super weird, even for me, for many years. Then I read more about it and tried it for myself and WOW. So, energy healing is based on the idea that our bodies operate on all these frequencies that we can tap into to promote our healing. Weird? Not so much. One study showed energy healing being as effective as physical therapy. UCLA now has a whole fucking LAB that studies electrical activity in the body. And UCLA is a state funded school. Tax money invested in energy healing. That's some serious street cred.

Reflexology focuses on applying pressure to areas of the ears, hands, and feet with the idea that these areas are connected to other points throughout the body (and polyvagal theory bears this out). Reiki (a Japanese term for *guided life force energy)* is the channeling of energy from a practitioner (or from one's own self) into the person who needs healing in order to activate the body's own healing process. These forms of energy healing (among others) help us find the stuck points in the body where we tend to hold our trauma, in order to better release them.

And BTW? Acupressure (tapping work like the EFT I talked about) is considered a form of energy healing as well as a form of acupuncture.

BIOFEEDBACK / NEUROFEEDBACK / ALPHA STIM TREATMENT

Biofeedback is the electronic monitoring of all bodily functions that help people learn to control responses that were previously automatic. Neurofeedback focuses specifically on the brain signals with the same intent to help individuals learn to manage their brain responses. We have far more control over our body and brain responses than we realize, and both bio and neuro can be great ways to augment or even speed up our unfuckening by giving us immediate feedback when our brain and body starts to get into fight, flight, and freeze mode. You essentially play a video game with your brain. It sounds as *Tron* as all-fuck, but you are set up with a Pac-Man type game or something similar, which you can only complete when you keep your brain waves in the optimal zone for your wellness. An example? My son did neuro work to help him with self-control and impulse management. Protocols were set in his game that helped him focus on that part of his brain. When winning the game, he actually felt the pressure of the blood rush to that section of his prefrontal cortex. And we could even see changes in his handwriting after just a couple of treatments!

I also include Alpha Stim treatment in this section, since even though it is a passive treatment, it falls under the same principles. Alpha Stims are designed to increase alpha brain waves (which are the great combination of calm and alert that we all crave). It works like neurofeedback, except the machine does the work for you rather than you training that brain state yourself. It helps with sleep, pain, anxiety, and a host of other conditions. I do use an Alpha Stim in my practice, especially when clients are working through a trauma narrative that is important to them, but causing a lot of "tough therapy day" hangovers. I have also had clients use them to have fewer symptoms in their daily lives without other medications. Alpha Stims have to be purchased with a prescription in the US, but any counselor can prescribe them like I do, not just a medical doctor.

NUTRITION CHANGES

When we are stressed we crave sugar like whoa. The brain needs glucose to maintain willpower and energy...which is why dieting is so hard. You are deprived of the glucose you need for willpower. Typically, the more stressed and busy we are, the worse we eat. So it's a vicious fucking cycle and ridiculously frustrating.

I know there are lots of nutrition wars out there. Figuring out the best plan for you can be exhausting (Paleo? Vegan? Gluten Free? THE FUCK I'M SUPPOSED TO EAT?). Short answer? Our body works best when we take care of it, eating the whole and healthy foods humans ate for centuries. And any diet you follow is going to make you more mindful of what you are putting in your mouth, for damn sure. So I'm not hell-bent on you choosing one over the other. In fact, everyone has differing dietary needs, which is why my cookbook (*The Revolution Will Include Cookies*, Say Something Real Press, LLC, 2016) offers variations in each recipe for some of the more popular ones.

And seriously, getting help from a clinical nutritionist, Chinese medicine practitioner, or trained naturopath who incorporates nutritional work can be well worth the investment. I do clinical nutrition work in my practice. I have worked with many people only once or twice on diet modifications and supplements and that's all they really needed: some basic assessments and advice to help them through the overwhelming information out there.

Nutrition and mental health really is a whole other book, but there are certain basics that can help enormously without getting into weird food-cult status.

- If we eat healthy about 85% of the time and enjoy treats about 15% we can maintain good functioning.
- Stay away from industrial foods as much as possible. The most important thing to remember about food labels? Trying to avoid foods that have labels. The more refined and machine-processed a food is, the more likely it is for your body to not recognize it.
- The movement away from gluten is more about the genetic modification of the wheat in the US and less about gluten itself, at least for most people (Celiacs and people with severe allergies aside). While moving to France or Italy would be ideal, the best thing we can do in the US is move away from gluten and genetically modified grains as much as possible. I live in South Texas so we live on corn tortillas anyway. Many individuals that are entirely grain free use coconut or almond flour. If you miss wheat like a physical pain, try the original einkorn wheat flour in your baking instead of the crap from the grocery store shelves.
- Many people who can't tolerate dairy do fine with raw milks. I can, my son can't. But it may be worth trying.
- Chemical sweeteners are total ass to your body. Aspartame, saccharine, sucralose? The ones that tend to come color coded

in yellow, pink, and blue? Cutting calories is not doing you any favor in the long run. A good calorie free sweetener option is stevia.

- If you suspect something is making you feel worse, try dumping it out for 21 days. See how you feel. Add it back in. Notice a difference? Your body will totally tell you what it needs.

PEER SUPPORTS

There is a huge body of research that shows that peer-to-peer support partners (as the federal agency SAMHSA refers to them) are an enormous part of many people's wellness and recovery processes. This makes sense. Someone who has similar lived experience has a level of empathy, understanding, and compassion that other people don't. There are phenomenally caring treatment providers out there, but we often connect to the people who have also traveled the same path we are on.

There are lots of names for this role in communities, including recovery coach, sponsor, family partner, and systems navigator, to name a few. There are also clinical professionals with lived experience who may share that experience as part of the work they do with people.

If peer supports are available wherever you are seeking treatment, give it a try. Someone who has been in the same hole you are in is sometimes the best person to talk to about finding the way out, doncha know?

NATURAL SUPPORTS

These are the people who love you just because you belong to them. Your family, your friends, teachers, coworkers, etc. that go above and beyond their role in your life to support you getting better. Having people who love us just because they DO is so, so, so important to getting better. Use them! If they ask to help, let them! It takes far more strength to accept help than to reject it. Be strong enough to allow others into your life.

CHOOSING THE RIGHT PROVIDER

This chapter is about a wide range of treatment options, not just your decision to choose the red pill or the blue pill. Along with all these options, it's also important to choose the right provider.

There is no magic way to do this, other than asking others for recommendations and feedback from people you know, asking the provider questions about their practice, and finding someone else if the fit isn't good.

Check out a potential provider's web presence as much as possible. Do you get a feel for them and their style? Feel comfortable with the idea of seeing them? Do they share a worldview on healing that matches your own?

Create a list of what is important to you in a treatment provider and your goals for treatment. If the work you are doing doesn't match

The important thing to remember about treatment is that it is *not* rent-a-friend. Treatment works when it is designed to help you process, heal, and move forward. If your time with this person becomes a time to perseverate and regurgitate rather than gain insight and release, it is doing more harm than good. Finding providers you like working with because they support you and guide you toward healing is vitally important. A good provider will not have their feelings hurt if you feel you will do better work with someone else. In fact, they should offer referrals and suggestions of who else you could connect with. The point of therapy is the getting better...not working with a particular person.

This is your care and your life. You don't owe your provider anything except payment for the services they provide.

PART TWO:

THIS IS YOUR
BRAIN ON LIFE

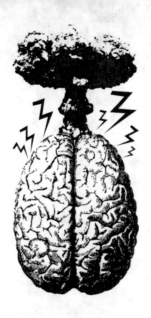

We are all cursed with living in interesting times. Even when shit is rocking along and our lives are generally positive, they are not curated for a focus on calmness, dullness, and space to think and chill. Remember when vacation was meant to be a time to have fun and adventures? Now it's a time to go away and sit somewhere and be as quiet, non-thinky, and non-doey as possible. I work with so many people who just need more time in their lives to chill. They aren't crazy, they are just fucking *exhausted.*

And this is an actual, real thing. We have a lot of physical illnesses, like Fibromyalgia, that might be better explained as adrenal fatigue. We may be getting a bit into woo-woo territory here, but it makes hella sense when you look at what's going on with the body during our stress response. Our adrenals secrete the hormones that help us react to *acute* stress. If these hormones end up on chronic demand because we are under *chronic* stress, it makes sense that hormonal production would start to taper off. While full-fledged adrenal insufficiency will show up in blood work, smaller declines in adrenal functioning won't.

But they may be showing up in other ways such as exhaustion, body aches, weird skin discolorations, loss of hair, lightheadedness with low blood pressure, etc. It's like the body becomes Miss Clavel from the *Madeline* books, announcing, "Something is not right."

But that's a whole other book. This is the brain book, after all. So yes, it is also quite-fucking-likely that our continued stress response (whether trauma-induced or not) is responsible for a shit-load of mental health diagnoses. Depression and other mood disorders, anxiety, anger, and addictions all have clear ties to the body's continued worn groove of a physical stress response.

Um, what? Keep your shit straight, lady. You just said stress hormones were secreted through the adrenals. So what the fuck does that have to do with mental and emotional health?

Excellent question, smarty pants! True story about the adrenals… BUT the adrenals (and all other glands) don't secrete anything until the pituitary gland (in the brain) says so. The adrenals (among others) may play the heavy, but it's under complete control of the pituitary. They may give the pounding but they didn't give the order for the pounding.

And who does the pituitary take orders from? Boom, back to square one.

The brain (specifically, the hypothalamus) is the actual master gland, the head coach. The head coach coordinates with the start quarterback, the pituitary gland, which then calls the plays for the whole rest of the team (hey there, body). The hypothalamus and the pituitary gland control the hormonal system AND the nervous system through their constant convos. All physical body regulation starts back in the brain.

So what's the magic answer, then? I wish I were the badass bitch who could tell you that. But as you well know, the real magic answer would be less stress. And that would be an utterly dick answer to give you...because that's not remotely possible most days, is it? So instead, we have to focus on better stress coping so we can manage our business without losing our minds and trashing our bodies.

This half of the book is the part of our mission (should you choose to accept) where we start looking at the specific ways our bodies and minds express stress. The great fuckening, if you will. Hang with me while I nerd out. I promise a lot of what you've been thinking, feeling, and doing is going to make epic amounts of sense.

ANXIETY

Don't you just love dictionary definitions? Anxiety is….*the state of being anxious.*

Well, no shit.

Interestingly enough, the word "anxiety" (and its definition of "being anxious") isn't one bit modern. In fact the word "anxious" was used MORE in the early 19th century than it has been in the early 21st.

You know what that means? Anxiety is a classic human condition that we have been grappling with for centuries. Modern living is sure as hell stressful. But modern life is not the source of human anxiety. Humanity in and of itself is an anxiety-provoking experience for so many people.

As a nerd is wont to do, I looked up the root of the word "anxious." It's from the Latin *anxius*, which is from the Ancient Greek *anko*, which means "to choke." Fucking word, they got that right.

Anxiety covers a lot of ground: It can be the experience of unease at its most chill. Distress at medium heat. Straight up panic at a full boil. And as those ancient Italians well knew, it's a hugely somatic experience. That is, it's something you feel in your body as much as it's something that controls your thoughts.

And it's always the most uncomfortable feeling ever. Your body is intentionally making you feel off balance so you have to attend to shit. There's a fancy term for that: Disequilibrium.

So here is our working definition: Anxiety is a state of full body disequilibrium at a level of intensity that demands immediate attention and corrective action on your part. It can be in the face of a real or perceived threat, either present or anticipated.

That right there is why anxiety is so hard to ignore. The whole point of the body producing that feeling is to demand your full attention like a naked, raging toddler running through the street in a snowstorm with a fist full of gummy bears in one hand and a bloody machete in the other.

Quite a visual right? Sure as hell not something you can readily disregard in the course of your day.

Anxiety demands every ounce of attention we have to give it, no matter how inconvenient the time or how unnecessary the anxiety actually was to begin with. So you can see how this relates to trauma reactions, right? It's really easy for anxiety to be our default setting if you have the kind of history that tells you to constantly be on guard.

SYMPTOMS OF ANXIETY

Thoughts and Feelings Symptoms

- Excessive worry
- Rumination (hamster wheel thinking patterns)
- Irritability/Anger (Weird, right? Anger is the culturally allowed emotion so we substitute that one a lot for what we are really feeling. Check out the anger chapter of this book!)
- Irrational fears/specific phobias
- Stage fright/social phobias
- Hyper self-awareness/self-consciousness
- Feelings of fear
- A sense of helplessness
- Flashbacks
- Obsessive behaviors, pickiness, perfectionism
- Compulsive behaviors
- Self doubt
- A sense that you are "losing it" or "going crazy"

Physical Body Symptoms [1]

- Trouble falling asleep or staying asleep
- Inability to rest

---

1 You are totally reading the physical body checklist and thinking…this is the same list for everything from anxiety to Ebola. Which is why so many people end up in emergency rooms thinking they are having a heart attack when they are having an anxiety attack. It's ALSO the same reason many people have missed the fact that they were having a heart attack because they were also having an anxiety attack. In Mental Health First Aid training, we suggest that if you see someone with potential anxiety attack symptoms, you ask them if they know what is going on and has it happened before. If they say "no" then treat it like the potential emergency situation it may be and call 911.

- Muscle tension
- Neck tension
- Chronic indigestion
- Stomach pain and/or nausea
- Racing heart
- Pulsing in the ear (feeling your heartbeat)
- Numbness or tingling in toes, feet, hands, or fingers
- Sweating
- Weakness
- Shortness of breath
- Dizziness
- Chest pain
- Stomach pain
- Feeling hot and cold (feeling like having chills and fever without running a temperature)
- Shooting pains/feeling like you have had an electric shock

Of course there are tons more symptoms. These are the more common ones and a complete list of all the things you may experience with anxiety would be an entire pamphlet of list-ness. You can find lots of great lists all over the interwebz, including ones that break down all the different categories of anxiety symptoms.

A lot of other things we do are adaptive to managing anxiety as well. Obsessive-Compulsive Disorder is totally an anxiety response. Cutting and other self-injury behavior may not stem from anxiety in all people, but does for many. So many diagnoses out there stem from just a few core issues. Anxiety is totally one of them.

But yeah. Anxiety symptoms. There is a lot of nasty shit our bodies do to us to get our attention and make us correct course.

Any of those hit home? You probably aren't reading this if the answer to begin with was "nah, I'm always chill."

Do I Have Anxiety or am I Just Anxious Sometimes?

You ask the most awesome questions! Like any other mental health issue, the answer lies in whether or not anxiety is controlling your life, rather than being a legit way of your body telling you to get off your ass and do something.

Clinically speaking, if you say it's a problem, I will agree that it's a problem. You know you the best.

Some people want a more formal way of self-check. There are a lot of anxiety assessment scales out there. The one you see quite often is the OASIS (which stands for Overall Anxiety Severity and Impairment Scale). It's well backed up by research and it's free to use, since it was developed by the National Institutes of Health (NIH).

OASIS doesn't have a magic cut-off number (as in: below this you are fine, above this you are batshit anxious). But it can be a good starting point for opening a conversation with a treatment provider or even just to reflect on your experiences.

The OASIS questions ask for you to reflect on your experiences over the past week and rate them on a scale of 0-4, with 0 being no probs,

1 being infrequent, 2 being occasional, 3 being pretty frequent, and 4 being constant fucking companion, thanks for the reminder.

Yeah, I'm translating a bit there. You can see the entire scale with the exact wording online, download it and print it if you want. microcosm.pub/oasis)

The exact questions themselves are as follows:

- In the past week, how often have you felt anxious?
- In the past week, when you have felt anxious, how intense or severe was your anxiety?
- In the past week, how often did you avoid situations, places, objects, or activities because of anxiety or fear?
- In the past week, how much did your anxiety interfere with your ability to do the things you needed to do at work, at school, or at home?
- In the past week, how much has anxiety interfered with your social life and relationships?

Having a "holy shit that's me!" moment? You are so not alone. The Kim Foundation notes that about 40 million American adults ages 18 and older (18.1% of people) in a given year meet the criteria for an anxiety disorder and 75% of individuals with an anxiety disorder had their first episode before age 21.

ANXIETY REALLY DOES SOUND A LOT LIKE STRESS

Yup, totally. And anxiety often comes from chronic stress. The big difference? Stress has external triggers. I know, I know, so does anxiety, but hang with me.

Stress can produce anxiety, but it can also produce a ton of other emotional responses (depression is probably the biggest). Anxiety is an internal response to stressors.

Think of it as a workflow process. If stress, then anxiety. Or any other number of uncomfortable emotional states. It all happens so fast it ends up mashed together in our brain. But there is definitely a cause and effect thing going on between the two.

A good book if you are interested in learning more about this is *Why Zebras Don't Get Ulcers* by Robert Sapolsky.

SO WHERE DOES THIS ANXIETY SHIT COME FROM?

Generally speaking, the human body works hard to maintain its chill point. So why is the body intentionally making you all bonkers-batshit with this anxiety thing? That makes as much sense as cheerfully banging your head into a brick wall, dunnit?

And once again, it all comes back to brain wiring. I am nothing if not on message.

Short version: We are wired to have strong emotional responses because those responses keep us alive. Feeling anxious is absolutely an important survival skill.

Longer version: If something triggers an anxiety response, your body gets flooded with norepinephrine and cortisol. Here's what those do:

Norepinephrine is released through your central nervous system (Hah! Nervous!) in order to prepare your body (which includes your brain) for action. It increases your focus and attention as well as your blood flow, blood pressure, and heart rate.

Cortisol is the classic stress hormone. It increases blood sugar and suppresses the immune system. Many people with chronic stress also gain weight, specifically as "belly fat," due to the constant cortisol production. The important thing to know here is that when cortisol is released with its partner in crime, norepinephrine, it creates strong memory associations with certain moods, to create warning signals of what you should avoid in the future.

The interesting thing here about anxiety as a stress response? The good thing? Anxiety means the body is still fighting back. This is fundamentally different from depression, which is essentially a wired response of learned helplessness (this is Robert Sapolsky stuff again).

Anxiety symptoms are active coping skills in the face of threat. The problem is only when the brain has decided that most everything, most everywhere is a threat. And, boom. That right there is a trauma response.

Even once you've figured out your triggers, anxiety isn't something you can willpower your way out of. As you saw, we have the asshole twin chemical combo going on. So in the here-and-now moment of anxiety or a straight up panic attack, you gotta do something to metabolize out those chemicals. When anxiety hits, you have to face it head-on.

Any of the exercises at the end of these chapters or in Chapter 4 can be used to help manage anxiety in the moment. Give your anxiety a goofy name or persona. Carry ice to hold as a reminder. Do some deep breathing exercises.

When you aren't feeling anxious, you can work on longer-term self-training to rewire your brain.

SELF-TRAINING FOR LEARNED OPTIMISM

Like all other brain retraining, there are certain things that can really help combat chronic anxiety. It isn't a magic bullet, better-immediately type cure, but the idea of training yourself to be optimistic has some merit behind it. There is a guy named Martin Seligman who is a legit big deal in my field. He was studying learned helplessness when he noticed that there are certain qualities that those obnoxiously, cheerful Susie-Sunshine optimistic people generally have:

Permanence: Optimistic people don't dwell on bad events, and approach them as temporary setbacks. If they get neg'd on, they bounce back more quickly. They also believe that good things happen for reasons that *are* permanent. Essentially, the world is fundamentally in their favor.

Pervasiveness: People who are happy monkeys tend to keep failure in its proper place. They recognize failure in one area as only belonging in THAT area, rather than meaning they are a failure at ALL THE THINGS ALL THE TIME. They also tend to let the things they are good at inform the rest of their lives, rather than keeping that in its own space. Sucking at basketball doesn't mean you will now make a shitty risotto. And if your risotto rocks, it is an indicator that YOU rock. And that you should cook more often. And invite me for dinner, I love risotto.

Personalization: Our cheerful buds blame bad events on bad circumstances rather than bad selfhood, but take credit for good circumstances as indicating that they are good people. So basically failures are events, not people. But successes are people, not events. If you dig me?

Interested in figuring out which way you wire? You can take the Learned Optimism test at *microcosm.pub/learnedoptimism*

Understanding what makes an optimist gave Seligman an idea. If we can learn *helplessness* and *pessimism*, then why can't we learn *optimism* and a *positive outlook*? Especially if we know the three big indicators we are shooting for?

TAKE ACTION: CHALLENGE YOUR NEG GREMLINS

Seligman created an ABCDE model designed to help you reframe your thinking as optimistic. And yes, it looks a ton like Albert Ellis' Rational Emotional Behavior Therapy (REBT) and Aaron Beck's Cognitive Behavior Therapy (CBT). We all borrow from each other's shit all the time. Therapists and researchers are assholes like that.

Think about the last time you felt anxious and write down some notes for each of these five letters:

In Seligman's model the A stands for Adversity. What bullshit is going down that generally triggers your anxiety response?

B stands for Belief. What are your beliefs about this event? Be honest, if your anxiety is triggered a lot, you are probably running a thought pattern in the direction of "THIS IS FUCKED!"

C stands for Consequences, though really it should stand for Cookie. Seligman didn't agree with me that once you think that shit's fucked you should go have a cookie. Instead, he wants you to look at how you reacted to the situation and to your beliefs.

D stands for Disputation. This is where you literally argue with the neg-gremlins your brain is throwing down and focus your attention on a new way of coping. Remember the storytelling brain? Create a new story to use instead.

And finally, E stands for Energization. What was the outcome of focusing your attention on a different way of reacting? Even if you were still pretty anxious, did you handle the situation better than you may have in the past? Over time, with doing this, do you notice that your anxiety is starting to fizzle out FINALLY?

To start with, just fill out the first three categories (A-B-C). Think back and look for examples of pessimism and negativity. Highlight those instances. Did you beat yourself up way more than you expected?

Give it a few days to sink in and then sit down with this list again and add the last categories (A-B-C-D-E). This is gonna be harder— this is active work to challenge that pessimism and teach yourself optimism instead. But you got this, rock star. It takes practice, stick with it!

1. Adversity: Just the facts, baby. Describe what happened (who, what, where, when) being as precise and detailed as you can.

2. Beliefs: What were you thinking? Like, exactly. What was your self-talk? Don't care if it was crude, ugly, or weird. Write it down. If it sparked a memory or flashback, that counts, too!

3. Consequences: How did these thoughts effect how you felt? How you behaved? What went on in your body? What emotions did you experience? How did you react?

4. Dispute:

There are four different ways you can dispute these negative beliefs

A. Evidence? Is there evidence that your belief was based in reality. If someone says "I hate you" then the belief that they hate you has some evidence behind it, right? But most beliefs really don't.

B. Alternatives? Is there another way you can look at this situation? What were the nonstatic circumstances (you don't always bomb a test, you were overtired from being sick)? What are the specifics (sucking at basketball doesn't make you a lame human being or even a lame athlete)? What did other's contribute to the situation (is it really ALL your fault???)?

C. Implications? Ok, so maybe you jacked up. Is it really a total catastrophe? What's some perspective you can add to this (ok, so I failed in that job interview…does that mean no one will hire me from now to infinity)?

D. Usefulness? Just because something is true, doesn't make it useful. How can you frame the experience as one that gives meaning to your life? Do you have a better respect for those things or people you value? Can you better demonstrate that respect now?

5. Energization:

How do you feel post disputation? Did your behavior change? Your feelings? Did you notice anything within the problem that you didn't notice before? Maybe even created a solution?

Now go celebrate your success here, hot stuff!

You can download a worksheet of the Adverse Event Log from my website at microcosm.pub/adverse

ANGER

If you have ever looked up a definition of anger, it tends to be not very helpful...usually a synonym rather than a definition. You read shit like that and you are thinking "No, no...I know what irritation is, antagonism is, rage is. They are all forms of anger. But what the fuck is anger actually made of?"

So anger is an emotion. Yeah, no shit. But bear with me. The word emotion derives from the Latin *emovere*, which means "out-move."

OK. NOW we are getting somewhere.

So, first off? General reminder:

> *Emotions are instinctive responses that are triggered by outside events and inside memories of past events. They function in the middle part of the brain, separate from the reasoning and cognitive processes in our pre-frontal cortex.*

So anger is an out-movement instinctive response. That makes sense, right? At its core, **anger is an instinctive response designed to protect us from harm by pushing us into concerted action.**

Boom. There we go. An operational definition of anger that is actually helpful.

Anger (and anger induced aggression) are activated in the same way that other emotions are. For anger, the specific activation triad is the amygdala, hypothalamus, and periaqueductal gray neural systems. Each type of threat activates these areas in different ways. Which is excellently geeky, but not so important to this convo.

The important thing to remember is that if we think we are at risk? Being threatened? We are going into brainstem fight club mode. Anger is how we prepare for that fight. The interesting part is that anger gets a lot of input from the PFC. All emotions do, obviously... but anger is pretty interesting in that the expression of it varies wildly in different cultures. Which means a lot of anger responses are taught, therefore PFC-negotiated. What's up with that?

A CULTURE OF ANGER

Why is everyone so fucking pissed off all the fucking time?

You don't have to look for a video on YouTube to see someone losing their shit. Just hang out at a grocery store, church parking lot, or mall food court for a little while and you will see someone flip the fuck out over something pretty damn minor in the grand scheme of things.

Maybe this person has been you at some point. Or someone you love. Or someone you barely tolerate but have to put up with.

There are a lot of theories about why we have all this anger, and they all make a lot of sense.

We are:

- Overdistracted
- Overstimulated
- Overcrowded, and
- Overinundated in everyday life.

Wouldn't anyone lose their shit?

But in plenty of other countries that are just as over-everything'd, you don't see nearly the same amount of anger responses as we do in the US and Europe. One Swedish researcher was fascinated by the cultural differences and compiled a review of studies about anger, comparing anger in the US, Japan, and Sweden and her findings were fascinating. She demonstrated that in Japan, for example, individuals are explicitly taught that there is an enormous difference between what you feel inside and how you present that to the world. It isn't something that Japanese citizens just pick up from those around them, but from the actual school curriculum.

In Japan, you are taught how to handle negative emotions.

But in contrast, when Americans are asked to explain uncomfortable emotions, they really have a hard time doing so. They often describe emotions as internal, not things that have consequences in behavior. But there is one interesting exception: Anger.

Anger, for some Americans, is considered a positive force of change that helps us overcome obstacles, cope with fear, and become more independent. One study found that 40% of individuals in the US considered their anger to have positive consequences over the long term.

That means that in the US, anger is not only acceptable at some level, it's often a GOOD thing.

And our cultural rules and values about anger are getting us in some serious fucking trouble.

- "I reached my boiling point!"
- "I was blowing off steam!"
- "I blew my stack!"
- "I was berserk!"
- "I went nuts!"
- "I unleashed my anger."

The underlying message in these symbolic explanations is that anger is in control of us, we are not in control of anger. Maybe that's why we love those movies where Liam Neeson kills everybody.

We speak of anger in a way that leads us to believe that anger is valid, it is in charge, and it must be acted upon. Our expectation is that anger requires retribution...and we see that our job, then, is to ensure a corrective response. From the time we are children, that anger is not only permissible, it's a positive means of addressing situations.

This isn't to say that anger is always bad, or always a negative force. No one has ever gained equal rights in this country by asking politely for them and having them handed over. And the energy that anger gives us can help us respond appropriately in certain situations.

If my children are in danger, my anger response will drive me to protect them. But my anger at the cashier for going on break after I finally get to the front of the line I've been waiting in? Probably not productive for anyone involved.

WHAT IS ANGER?

Anger, like all emotions, isn't good or bad or right or wrong.

It just IS.

Emotions are information, designed to help us make decisions that will protect us and keep us safe. They are triggered in the middle part of our brain, in our amygdala, based on the information we are processing and our memories of past situations.

Positive emotions are a type of "carry on" feedback. Our brains telling us "Yes! Yes all cookies! Yes hiking with friends! Yes funny movies! These things feel nice, let's do all these things!"

Negative emotions are the polar opposite. They are the cat scrunched up in the corner, ears flattened and growling. "No! Do not want! Does not feel good or safe or nice at all! Make it stop!"

Anger triggers the fight/flight/freeze response.

Feeling some serious fucking anger is a normal part of being a human being. Losing your shit is not.

As I tell my clients…you are allowed to BE crazy, but you aren't allowed to ACT crazy.

Being as irritated as fuck because someone jacked the parking spot you were waiting for?

Totally legit.

Going postal over it? Not so helpful.

Not so helpful to everyone around you, not so helpful to greater society, and…for purely selfish reasons…not so helpful to you.

When we lose our fucking minds on a regular basis, we are wiring our brains into a constantly heightened state that eventually fries our circuits (and pushes away everyone we love in the process). We program ourselves to always be on the alert. So we react with far greater speed than we used to, and perceive more situations as being dangerous, hostile, or threatening. We are constantly jumping at shadows.

Our brains never get to rest and recharge and we start struggling with many other conditions associated with this wiring change. Added up, those conditions are known as **autonomic nervous system dysfunction**. Many common health problems (heart disease, high blood pressure, food allergies) as well as many common mental health issues (depression, anxiety, PTSD) are related to a continued heightened response.

And back to anger right here, because anger is the worst offender in this regard.

To borrow a famous Buddhist expression, anger is like holding onto a hot coal and expecting the person we are angry at to get burned.

ANGER IS A SECONDARY EMOTION

And you know what is REALLY fucked up about anger? This emotion that we culturally believe is driving us to success? It isn't even a primary emotion.

I know, you are now asking: And what the FUCK is that supposed to mean, fancy PhD lady?

It means that while anger may be the first emotion we recognize at some level in ourselves, and the emotion we act (or react) upon, I guarantee you it actually isn't the first thing you feel in any given situation. Anger is a secondary emotion.

The best model I have seen to explain anger uses the acronym AHEN.

AHEN is as simple a conceptualization as you can get.

ANGER is triggered by

- Hurt
- Expectations not met
- Needs not met

Of course, it is a little more complicated than that in that we aren't usually limited to just one of these triggers but a big glob-ball of all of the above.

Here's how to use AHEN. Next time you are pissed as all get-out, ask yourself the following questions:

1) **Am I hurt?** Did something happen here that made me feel insecure? Unsafe? Unvalued? Unworthy? Unappreciated? Just plain old sad as fuck? Of all the things that have kicked me in the nuts over the years, why is this situation particularly nasty? Was it the person who I perceive as doing the hurting? Is it a particular situation that bothers me more than others? Has this been a problem for me in the past? Is this one of those fucking TRIGGERS people yammer on about?

Break this shit down…why the hurt?

2) **Did I have expectations that were not met?** Was my little brain bopping along expecting a certain thing to happen and it didn't happen? Was that a realistic expectation? (Be honest here, aiight????) If it was realistic, is it some life changing shit when it didn't happen? Someone took the parking spot you got to first. Dick move. Reasonable expectation that they would follow civilized parking lot protocol? Fuck yeah. Otherwise we are 3 inches away from complete social chaos…people need to follow some fucking rules, FFS. But is it life changing? Not so much. You find another parking spot (eventually) and get parked (eventually). Then, hopefully, you move on. So break this shit down next. Was it a reasonable expectation to begin with? Did the world fucking end because it wasn't met? Some shit is for-real serious, some isn't. Tell yourself the truth here. Is this an expectation worth getting all hurt over?

3) **Did I have needs that were not met?** This is a tough one. Because how do you define what a need really is? If you are Buddhist, you may not think they exist at all, right? On an

existential level you are all kinds of right. But on a physiological level, the brain is wired to keep you alive. If something threatens the brain's sense of equilibrium, you are gonna get flooded with FIGHT BACK chemicals, straight to the amygdala.

Certain things are going to trigger this fight response more than others. Imminent danger is a DUH. We need to feel safe. We need to perceive our loved ones as safe. If your brain perceives a threat to you, your sweetie, your kids, your pooch? It's ON. Protect what's important to you! Get MAD!

There are other kinds of safety needs we can't discount. Human beings are hardwired for relationships. We need the stability of relationships in order to be well. Our brains know this, even when society tells us "You don't need no one but your own DAMN SELF, playa'!" That's some bullshit. We live communally not because we are overcrowded but because we have to do it to survive. So with that need comes the need for emotional safety. We need to feel secure and supported in our relationships with other people. We need to have a good idea of what to expect. We need to feel loved. This is more than some dickwad jacking our parking space. This is about our fundamental human need to feel supported by others in the world. We need to know that we are safe with the people we love, that they love us back, and that they are not going to hurt us, at least not intentionally.

We need to get out of dark alleys at 2AM. We need to get away from the erratic driver swerving next to us on the freeway. But we also need a community of people who love us silly and make us feel secure.

The anger that kicks us in the ass for the longest is when that contract gets broken. When the person with whom we most needed to be safe did something that questioned that safety.

You can see why I have stuck with this model of understanding anger for years now, I'm sure. It helps make sense of so many of the situations we have to navigate on a daily basis.

Knowing where anger comes from is way more than half the battle. It's like 90% of it.

How many times have you had an "Oh!" moment when you realized why you felt a certain way and then the feeling just…melted?

And then there is the other 10% of the time.

Shit be real and managing it is hella hard.

But like we talked about above, dealing with anger is like dealing with any other piece of information that we need to take into account to resolve a situation. It isn't a good or bad thing and it doesn't have to be the driving force of our decisions.

TAKE ACTION: WHERE DOES YOUR ANGER COME FROM?

When was the last time you were angry? When you aren't in actual imminent danger or under actual threat, and after you've used the AHEN model to break some shit down, evaluate the following questions:

1) What are the underlying roots of your anger? Once you figured them out, were they legit or were they more about you and your history than about the present situation? If you aren't sure, reflect on when you first noticed that you were angry. What was going on around you...sights, smells, noises, people? What were you doing? What were others doing? What were you thinking about? Any particular memories coming up at that time?

2) If the roots are legit, are they something that need to be addressed or is it one of those bullshit daily life things that just happens? Speeding ticket, fucked up drive thru order, etc.?

3) If it needs to be addressed what is the best way to do so? How do you correct the situation with as little disruption as possible? What can you do to keep from getting further hurt in the process (physically, emotionally, and mentally)? Can you keep the hurt to others minimal (physically, mentally, and emotionally)? Does it need to be addressed immediately, or can it wait until you are calmer and feel safer? Is there anyone else you can talk to that is going to have a healthy, supportive perspective...a counselor, friend, mentor, family

member? Someone who knows you, loves you, and will totally call you out on your shit if need be?

4) After you act (instead of react), then evaluate the results. Did it work? Is this a strategy that you can use again? Are you still angry or are you feeling better and safer now?

ADDICTION

Let's start with one universal truth right off the bat.

Practically everyone is addicted to something, at some point in their lives.

Yep, quite possibly you. Definitely me. If you picked up this book with the intent of helping someone you care about, one of the first things you can do is recognize your own struggles with some form of addiction.

Yeah, I know that seems a seriously dick thing to say. But bear with me for a second, this is gonna make sense.

The spelling of the word "addict" is unchanged from the first use of it in the mid 16th century. It was used to describe someone who was *bound* or *devoted*. Still dead-on now, innit?

Addiction was originally defined by early mental health professionals (Freud and the like) and the first peer recovery group facilitators (AA and the like) based on what they saw, heard, and could measure at the time. Consensus was that addiction is a function of cravings plus compulsive use.

It was a simple model, and was our first start in providing addiction treatment. But it really didn't encompass all the things addiction can be, especially in light of more recent neuroscience research.

While our understanding is by no means complete, we now know that addiction is WAY more than craving plus use. The neurobiology of addiction is epically complicated, though new research is starting to give us different insights than we have had in the past. We know that substance addictions set off the pleasure pathways in the brain like WHOA…although at different levels for different people. Which helps explain why some people are more prone to substance addiction while others find that the same substances make them feel fucking awful. We also know that the anticipation of use can set off all kinds of dopamine signals in the brain…which totally explains addictive behaviors where a mind altering substance isn't being used at all.

Gabor Maté, in his book *In the Realm of Hungry Ghosts*, offered this definition of addiction, which I have used ever since I read it, even in my dissertation.

"Addiction is any repeated behavior, substance-related or not, in which a person feels compelled to persist, regardless of its negative impact on his life and the lives of others.

Addiction involves:

1.) Compulsive engagement with the behavior, a preoccupation with it

2.) Impaired control over the behavior

3.) Persistence or relapse despite evidence of harm

4.) Dissatisfaction, irritability, or intense craving when the object—whether it be a drug, activity, or other goal—is not immediately available."

Some addictions are clear. The homeless woman with the fresh track marks over years of scars. The man who loses his home and car to gambling debts and now is hiding from dangerous creditors.

Some addictions are softer, easier to engage in and still get up and function every day. Those of us who take out a bag of chips or tray of muffins after a tough day. Or go shoe shopping for our 8th pair of black sandals that we are never going to wear.

There are addictions that excuse us from society altogether, those that keep us barely afloat within it, and those that become a barrier between us and the rest of the world. It's only a matter of degree, in the end.

How do we define when we cross over into addiction territory? As a relationally-trained therapist, my answer is a simple one. *When our addiction becomes our primary relationship.* Maybe not in our hearts and heads. But in our behaviors, definitely. When we don't have control over our addictions, we are spending time, resources, and energy on the addiction instead of the people we love. And instead of, let's face it...*ourselves*.

WHERE ADDICTIONS COME FROM

Where do addictions come from? And why the fuck do I say that practically everyone is some kind of addict?

When we engage in an addiction to the point of it taking precedence over our relationships with people, it's a problem. It's a coping mechanism that has moved from soothing us to controlling us completely.

Addiction is the domain of the sensitives. The empaths. The people who notice early on what is dark, hidden, and broken in society. We learn that pointing out these discrepancies is grounds for punishment. We are told that good boys and girls don't notice such things. And if they do, they CERTAINLY don't talk about it. So we start taking on responsibility for all this shit that is dark and broken. We swallow it down and it starts eating us alive. Everything must be our fault. We clearly aren't good people. Relationships aren't safe. The only way to get through is with a mechanism of coping and support.

If you have had a trauma, if you have been hurt so badly in a way that you don't trust the world, you are far, far, far more likely to be susceptible to addictive behavior.

At some point in most people's lives, we start using something to help us feel better. We are hungry for something that we aren't getting. So we start feeding that need with other stuff. Substances, behaviors, activities. Whatever we choose probably helps for a while. It soothes the raw hunger that we are feeling, and helps us forget about what we really need.

In reality, addictions are just coping skills gone awry.

There is a huge, grey, fuzzy margin between healthy coping and addiction. It's a big, blurry area where we start losing control over our coping skill, be it a substance, an activity, or a behavior, and it starts controlling us and taking over more and more of our lives.

Coping skills are intended to help us stay grounded and get through difficult times. They aren't intended to replace reality, or replace our real relationships. So when we can't entirely be with the people we love... When we can't entirely feel safe within ourselves... That means whatever we are using to get us through is operating as an addiction.

HOW WE HEAL

There are two basic categories for addictions treatments. The traditional model of addiction treatment is abstinence based. That is, you cannot engage in the addiction at all...that's the only mechanism of healing. The other is harm-reduction. This method is more of a negotiation with the addiction, finding ways to reduce the harm that is occurring in our use. Let's talk about how some of these treatments might work in practice.

ABSTINENCE BASED TREATMENT

I grew up within the framework of AA: Alcoholics Anonymous. My father is in recovery, so we spent enormous amounts of time at AA meetings, events, conferences, and having our house full of people new in their sobriety. AA was unique when it was created some 80 years ago. The idea is of people with lived experience sharing their support and helping others on the path to finding their own sobriety. It's based in giving yourself over to a higher power, whatever that happens to be for you. Many people who struggle with faith-based services are uncomfortable with this framework. And other prescriptive elements have emerged in some groups that feel exclusionary. For instance, many groups believe that sobriety means no mind-altering substances, even medications for a mental health disorder.

It's a shame because the AA model also can be of great benefit to healing. Higher Power? For some people that may just be the greater community surrounding you. Healthy relationships, attunement to your own authentic voice. It doesn't have to be an omnipotent God of some form. And you shouldn't have to give up the medications that are keeping you sane while letting go of the addictions that sent you on the road to crazy.

And there are plenty of groups that do honor those differences in beliefs, whether it be AA, NA, OA, DDA, or any other twelve-step model program. There are meetings available online 24 hours a day, and in most communities throughout the world. There are meetings that focus on special groups of individuals who may not be comfortable in general meetings, such as Lambda AA, which was created for LGBT individuals in recovery and the Wellbriety movement, which focuses on the specific needs of indigenous individuals.

There are other plans outside the traditional twelve-step model that are also abstinence-based, such as SMART Recovery, Save Our Selves/Secular Organizations for Sobriety (SOS), and Women for Sobriety. These programs have also been around for some time, but focus on newer research about making sobriety effective. These programs generally also have more of a focus on self-efficacy/internal locus of control rather than relationality/higher power support.

That's a simplification, but my point is that there are sober living options outside of the twelve-step model. And a variety of options mean a larger chance of finding something that makes sense for you.

HARM REDUCTION

There are two times when harm reduction treatment is the best treatment bet:

1) When it is what you HAVE to do.
2) When it is what you WANT to do.

So, here's the thing. Some addictions can be given up entirely and recovery can be achieved through total abstinence. One can live forever without drinking alcohol or purchasing a lottery ticket, after all.

But sometimes we don't have any fucking choice about abstinence. Food addiction? Still gotta eat every day. Most work addicts aren't independently wealthy to where they can just quit their job and instead go meditate at an ashram in support of their recovery.

Sex addiction? While I suppose you could make the argument that abstinence is an appropriate treatment strategy, I haven't yet worked with anyone that would agree that giving up sex was an option. And considering most of them had long-term partners, their partners wouldn't agree either.

What's more, some people do not WANT to let go of the substance or behavior that is the source of their addiction. For example, someone sex positive may want to continue to use porn that is conscious and affirming, without having their use of porn take control of their lives. Or they may want to use substances in a controlled way, rather than in a way that is impacting their lives in a negative manner.

And yeah, I get it. Some addictions are so insanely dangerous that abstinence is likely the only thing that will save your life. Crack cocaine? Not something you want to try to use in moderation.

But most abstinence-style recovery programs do not allow for a harm reduction detox—or the use of less harmful substances to mitigate the effects of not using the harmful ones. For example, there has been enormous debate surrounding the use of methadone (legal) and marijuana (legal in some states) to support recovery from hard drugs.

Some substances require a medical detox (alcohol and heroin being the two big ones) to prevent serious medical complications or even death. Detox is not the same thing as addiction treatment and recovery, of course. It's only meant to get you through the medically dangerous part of getting rid of the poison in your system so you CAN move on to treatment and recovery.

Of course, some substances are just a bitch to detox, even if they don't involve medical risk. Anyone who is a caffeine addict knows how bad it feels when you don't get your fix. Refried ass is an apt term.

Straight detox (whether inpatient medical detox or chaining yourself to the bed and away from the coffee pot) can be a huge barrier for many people. While there are more and more medical programs that are no-fee, these programs obviously can't make up for lost wages during the stay, provide childcare, etc.

For all these reasons and more, harm reduction is becoming a more frequent treatment option for many people.

There are formal, nation-wide programs like Moderation Management. And there are lots of treatment professionals who use a wide variety of harm reduction strategies in their practice as part of therapy. And yes, I am absolutely one of those treatment professionals.

Instead of thinking that you have to be completely abstinent before digging into the emotional stuff, I believe that addictive behavior is a way people manage their traumas, and that we need to work on the underlying trauma and find other ways to cope with it before we take away that coping skill. Until the addiction becomes the least helpful coping skill that someone has, it's going to be hella hard to treat.

UNFUCK YOUR ADDICTION

So here is what I ask clients to do instead.

This is clearly the world according to Dr. Faith. I am no more right or wrong than anyone else, but I have been doing this work for a very long time and have found ways of supporting recovery that work best for the individuals I work with and my own worldview/ treatment style.

Now, anyone who says they have the BEST way to treat addiction is a fucking liar. I would never claim such nonsense. So take my suggestions for only what they are—suggestions. Use anything that works for you and dump the rest.

1. Consider addiction's rightful place in your life as being a replacement relationship.

Shit ends up in the addiction zone when it starts replacing our authentic relationships with the people around us and with our own self. We become in service to the substance or behavior that is the point of our addiction. It isn't just something in our life, it becomes the most important thing in our life. Addiction recovery is a recognition of that. Maybe you don't feel that you have any relationships worth saving. Maybe you don't even think that YOU are worth saving. I'd beg to differ, but it's not up to me. I would suggest, gentle reader, that you give space to the possibility that there are good relationships out there to be had. And your current addiction is a nasty, dirty bitch who is never gonna love you back the way you deserve to be loved. When you are hanging out with your addiction, consider what needs are being met and if this is really the ideal way of handling them. Once we become conscious of our engagement with the addiction and remind ourselves we are choosing the addiction over ourselves and over others, it becomes harder and harder to continue to make that choice. Don't step into your usage without being mindful of what you are doing. It gets harder and harder to fuck over yourself and the people you love when you are doing it with intentionality and ownership.

2. You're in charge of yourself. You really are. Even if you feel that you aren't. Even if you feel that you never have been.

Ultimately, your use will change because *you want it to*. You will change because you want to be better, because you want your relationships to be better. Even if you get remanded by a court into treatment, whether or not you stay sober will ultimately be up to how badly you want to, right? No matter what people tell you to do, whether or not you do it is ultimately up to you. Remind yourself that when you feel yourself bristling against authority. What do YOU want for yourself? Is what you are doing getting you there?

3. It's far easier to START doing something new than STOP doing something old.

A lot of really great clinicians are fearful of working with individuals with addictions because they think the idea is to get someone to stop doing something. I take the opposite approach, focusing on adding healthier behaviors and building healthier relationships rather than focusing on the addiction itself. We may build awareness around some of the history and/or behaviors surrounding use, but we don't generally focus on the use itself. If you build a healthier you, the addiction often becomes less and less needed as a coping skill. I was asked recently *"How often does therapy consist of just getting people to get out more?"* And the answer is? A helluvalot!!! You don't have to go balls to the walls superhealthypants, but can you add in one small thing that makes you feel better instead of worse every day? And can you pay attention to how you feel when doing THAT thing instead of the addiction thing?

4. Remember that sobriety and recovery are spectrums.

You get to choose the best point for yourself on that spectrum and you get to choose when that changes. Do abstinence if that works for you. Do taper and harm reduction if that works better. Part of your journey is figuring out who you are and who you can be in relation to your addiction. I have worked with people who soon learned that playing a game of poker would spiral into heroin use within a month. Only complete abstinence kept them safe. Then I have worked with other people who tapered hard drug use with marijuana. A few gave up the marijuana too at a later point (it isn't legal in the state I live in, so using had some inherent legal risk) and some continued to use marijuana instead of other drugs successfully for years with no relapse. As alluded to in mentioning the legality of marijuana in my state? You are, of course, responsible for all the consequences of your behavior. For example, if you are mandated to go in for drug screenings and you pop hot, you can't blame this book.

5. Stop the bullshit.

With yourself, with others. Blowing smoke up people's asses, convincing yourself that you are making good decisions when you know very fucking well that you aren't? Stop that. You may not have had much control over your life up until this point but consider this my permission slip to you to TAKE IT BACK. Accountability through and through. If you engage in your addiction, own it with honesty. Don't blame anyone else. Remind yourself that your engagement in your addiction is a choice you are making. Make it consciously. Instead of telling yourself *"my partner broke up with me so it's their fault I'm using, I just can't handle all this,"* try *"My partner broke up with me and that triggered all my struggles with abandonment. I'm choosing to use because it's coping skill that has worked best for me and trying something new feels overwhelming."* You may find it harder to hurt yourself with your addiction when you take a mindful sense of responsibility for it.

6. Figure out your triggers.

If you squeeze your eyes shut, you will continue to bump into shit. If you keep your eyes open to the terrain, you can start putting together a map. When you catch yourself doing the thing, ask yourself to retrace what led to it. The HALT acronym is a big one in addiction treatment...am I hungry? Angry? Lonely? Tired? If you pair awareness triggers with accountability for your actions it becomes increasingly hard to stay on the addiction path.

7. Forgive yourself your fuck-ups.

You are a fuck-up. So am I. Yaaay for being human. Have some self-compassion for that fact. Self-compassion is the opposite of self-esteem. It's about your insides rather than your successes and failures on the outsides. It means you forgive yourself your failures and your human bumbling. And no, this doesn't mean you get to be a hedonistic fuck-face. In fact, if you are aware of your human frailty, and take care of yourself in the moments where you are your most fragile and off-kilter, research shows you actually take *more* responsibility and accountability for your actions. Kristen Neff wrote an amazing book called *Self-Compassion*. Read the thing if you haven't. Changed my life.

8. And forgive the fuck-ups done unto you.

I hear you. Some terrible shit has happened to you. Seriously awful stuff. Awful stuff will continue to happen. Sometimes people are just as balls as can be. Forgiveness isn't about them, it's about how much bullshit you want to carry around with you. I'm guessing not that fucking much. Forgiveness doesn't mean allowing ongoing dickitude. Instead, it will help you set better boundaries so you know how to better protect yourself in the future. And it will open the door to more real conversations with the people around you, instead of continuing to only converse with your demons.

9. Anticipate your continued imperfect humaning.

Do your best to do your best. But seriously. You're gonna fuck up. You may even relapse. And you know what? We either win or we learn. So take the fuck-ups as new ways of getting good information about yourself. What did you do differently this time? What can you take from this experience and do differently next time? Honoring our fuck-ups with clarity is brave as fuck. And you so have the capacity for epic bravery.

TAKE ACTION: WHERE CAN YOU SAY YES?

Addiction is often treated like a lack of willpower. Nancy Reagan told us it was simple enough...all you have to do is *just say NO*.

So that becomes our internal dialogue. Why can't we, sometimes? Why can't we just say no? It leads to a shame spiral and blocks our ability to be self-compassionate.

If addictions are replacing other relationships, that's where our first steps in healing should begin.

So sit down and make a list:

What can you say "yes" to?

Not as a replacement for your addiction. Not instead of or a giving up of something else. Life isn't a zero sum game, after all. And being told to give up the thing that has helped you the most in the past isn't fair. I know that's your end goal, of course. But we don't have to start there if you aren't ready.

Just say yes to something new. Something you used to love but don't do anymore. Something you always wanted to try.

Expand the boundaries of your life back out by adding something. What happens? What shifts? What else do you need now? What do you no longer need?

DEPRESSION

Depression is one of those words we throw around and use as a label so indiscriminately it's lost its meaning. I've been guilty of it and I bet you have, too. I used the word *depressed* to express how I felt when Whole Foods stopped carrying my favorite ginger cookies, even though *pissed as fuck with a preposterous sense of entitlement* would have been a way better description of my state of mind.

Depression is not your team losing in overtime, losing your favorite watch, getting fired, or breaking up with a partner. Granted all of these things have different levels of suckitude, but at their core they are all losses that cause understandable levels of grief (which is the topic of the next chapter). Grief and loss can absolutely be traumatic, and can absolutely lead to depression. But with proper space and time to heal, we heal. Depression is a far more insidious problem. And sometimes it doesn't have anything to do with an identifiable loss.

Just like anxiety, depression is related to the biochemistry of stress.

Anxiety is an over-response to stress hormones. It's the body trying to go into survival mode to protect itself, based on what it thinks to be true. *Anxiety is a biochemical over-response to stress.*

Depression is the body's way of saying *nothing I do is going to help anyway, it all sucks ass no matter what. Depression is a biochemical learned helplessness response to stress.*

Depression is the body's way of saying *if nothing I do makes any difference, there is no point in enjoying ANYTHING.* Robert Sapolsky defines depression as "a genetic-neurochemical disorder requiring a strong environmental trigger whose characteristic manifestation is an inability to appreciate sunsets." I define it as **a clinical case of the fuck-its.**

In his book *Tribe*, Sebastian Junger writes about depression in relation to anger in how it is triggered as part of the fight-flight-freeze response. If anger is preparing you to fight, then depression is your brain's way of turtling up...to not get noticed, to not be too active, to not do the things that might put you in more danger.

Depression is not the same thing as sadness, grief, coping with trauma, or coping with loss. Depression is the complete shutdown of all the things that make being human a joyful experience. The biggest, most consistent symptom of depression is *anhedonia*, which is a tongue-twister way of saying *an inability to feel pleasure*. If you look at that word, you can see it essentially means not-hedonistic. If you struggle with depression, you have all kinds of feels. Guilt, shame, anger, irritability, hopelessness, overwhelming grief. But you rarely have experiences of pleasure, gratitude, connectedness, and joy. And if you do reach out for them, you feel them snatched away more often than not. Depression is the thief of all the wonderful things that make human-ing worth it.

The word depression comes from the Latin word *deprimere,* which means *to press down.* Yup, exactly. Depression operates as a literal anchor into the muck. An actual diagnosis of Major Depressive Disorder requires that anhedonia be present every day for at least two weeks. Other symptoms that are also really, really common are:

- Low energy/fatigue
- Low level chronic pain
- Jacked up concentration, difficulty making decisions
- Feeling guilty and/or worthless
- Sleeping a ton or sleeping for shit (whether not sleeping at all, or sleeping badly)
- Feeling either super restless, or really slowed down (like moving underwater or brain wrapped in cotton)
- Intrusive thoughts of death (morbid ideation) or suicide (suicidal ideation)
- Change in eating habits (and five percent or more change in weight either up or down because of it)
- Irritability, anger, low distress tolerance

HOW DOES THE GETTING BETTER PART WORK, THEN?

The bad news is there is no magical path for healing depression. However, that's ALSO the good news. That means you get to find the path that works best for you. And fuck anyone who tells you that you aren't healing correctly. Because there is no magical answer about what treatments you should seek out. The important thing is to be aware of the many options available for you to choose from... especially when there are people who are going to try to push their worldview about treatment on you.

Only more recently have mental health professionals started to incorporate trauma-informed care in their word. If depression is predisposition + trigger, then wouldn't it make sense to look at some of the possible triggers? We've already covered all this, I know. But as a general reminder?

Very little of our genetic programming is set in stone. Two to five percent of all diseases TOTAL are related to a single faulty gene. However many, many, MANY diseases are lurking in our DNA and can be turned on by the right conditions. The shiny-human super fancy term for this is *epigenetics*.

Whoa, wait a fuckin' minute here, Doc. Does this mean that my depression that was turned on could turn back off again?

My pain in the ass therapist answer is: *That's a hard maybe.*

If you know or at least have a hardcore suspicion that your mood disorder has a big-assed trauma taproot then it might make a fuck-ton of sense to treat the trauma along with the other symptoms.

Whoa, lady, does this mean I may not to be on meds forever? Maybe I won't pass it down to my kids? Maybe it won't keep getting worse year after year like it has been?

More *hard maybe* answers there. Blech. I wish I knew the magical equations in that regard. I can tell you that people tend to have a way better handle on their mood disorders if we unpack the trauma fuckery. They manage present and future triggers way better. Sometimes they aren't nearly as impacted. At the very least they know to go "Shit just got real again, I need some Buddha-damn help right about now." If they are on meds, they are often able to at least decrease, or find ways of not having to increase year in year out like they have been.

And yes, I have seen complete remission of symptoms a number of times. It is possible.

People don't need to unconsciously perpetuate the cycles of trauma in their own kids, either. They teach them the healthy coping skills that they have learned. (Great book? *Trauma Proofing Your Kids* by Peter Levine) And if their kiddos end up struggling as well, they are the first to advocate for help immediately and early to keep them from struggling through the system. And they aren't going to allow any bullshittery from the school system and the mental health system as they get that help. Because no fucking way are they gonna let their kids suffer the way they did.

This is another one of those tough-subject topics, I realize. It's hard to be cheerful about an illness that tends to eat people alive. But like everything else, I really believe that understanding the biochemical roots of the problem is enormously helpful in feeling less trapped and crazy. You are not defined by your depression. You are not weak, and you didn't do anything wrong. You didn't deserve this.

You are not being punished. You hit the perfect storm of genetics + trigger and you are now dodging and weaving while running your ass off toward getting better.

People struggling with depression (or any mental illness) are ANYTHING but crazy.

They are survivors, fighting back against brain chemistry that is entirely at odds with all the things that make life worth living. Those of you who are living this? Who are saying *"Fuck you, Depression, you don't get to win today"*?

You are the bravest people I know.

Keep fighting.

ACTIVITY: WHAT I WANT BACK

Depression's fundamental difference from sadness is how much it steals from us when it strikes. It's like a police state where not just behaviors are punished, but crimes of thought as well. Depression takes away our lives and our **will** for life.

Have you ever been in this place? Are you in this place now?

I would love for this to be the time that you pick up the phone and start asking for help. Help from families and friends, help from professionals. But I know how hard it is to make that call…and how hard it is to actually get the help you are begging for. It feels

I also know that if you are reading this book and have gotten this far, that's where you are headed. You are starting to get a glimmer of a thought of "Fuck this shit, I want my life back."

And if I am right? What do you most want back? Of all the things that make life worth living that depression has robbed you of, what are you missing the most right now? It may not be the biggest thing, and that's OK. In fact, it's great because it may be easier to wrestle it away.

You don't have to do anything about this yet, unless you want to. But the intent of this exercise is to start with the *thought crime* that depression has forbidden you from having. The thought that you can do better and deserve to do better. The thought that there is a world out there that you have the right to participate in and maybe even enjoy.

Let's start right there. Write those thoughts down. Remember that world. That's the beginning of your new story.

THE IMPORTANCE OF HONORING GRIEF

Remember how we talked about the trauma recovery timeline? While there is no magic number associated with the time we need to heal, researchers have found that ninety days is the basic timeframe for reestablishing equilibrium. And the first thirty days are the most fragile and necessary part of that process. When something disrupts that experience, we are far more likely to experience long-lasting symptoms of trauma, which can look like depression, anxiety, or any number of mental illness labels.

Part of avoiding a trauma response is having the space to grieve. Grieving what hurt you. Grieving for what you lost. Grieving the life that you wanted that isn't the same now.

Mental illnesses like depression and anxiety have strong genetic predispositions, but research also shows that they still require a triggering event. Unresolved grief often acts as exactly that trigger. Not having the space to heal can create actual biochemical changes in our brains.

It's also not too late, you know. It doesn't matter if it's been thirty days or thirty years. For many people, healing an established trauma response may include going back and doing the grief work you were never allowed in the first place. Grief scares the fuck out of us, whether it is our own or someone else's. It feels like a freefall that is completely dark and completely bottomless.

When we don't allow or aren't allowed our grief process, this can often lead to an experience of "traumatic grief." That is a level of unresolved grief that turns into mental illness. Let's work to stop that bullshit and focus on honoring grief.

That starts with how we talk about it, how we support others who are grieving, and how we ensure we get the support we need in our own healing processes. Grief is the fundamental process of letting go. In her book *How Can I Help?* June Cerza Kolf notes the statistic that the number one fear experienced by human beings is the fear of abandonment. C. S. Lewis, in his book in *A Grief Observed* stated:

"No one ever told me that grief is so much like fear."

Grief is a realization of the certainty of abandonment. It is our worst fear made reality.

It makes sense, then, that we don't really talk much about grief. It scares us shitless. We fear that discussing it will somehow invoke it. While we know at an intellectual level that abandonment is unavoidable throughout our human existence on the planet, it still knocks us sideways when it happens.

When we discuss grief, our first thought is always of death. But grief is the experience of any kind of loss, any type of abandonment in our lives. Grief can come with the loss of a job, the loss of a relationship (through any means, not just death), or the loss of a way of life we have come to know and expect. We can grieve changes even if they are happy ones. Getting married can be an amazing thing, but we may still grieve the loss of our single days. Becoming an adult is something we all looked forward to, until that moment we had to grieve the freedom of childhood and the ability to hand over decisions to someone else.

Our cultural expectation is to possess rather than release. Loss (abandonment) is a forced release for which we have few mechanisms to heal ourselves or support healing in others. We don't talk about the inevitable *letting go* of that which we think we possess.

WHAT IS GRIEF?

Grief means, most simply, *deep sorrow*. The word grief comes from the old French *grever*, which means "to burden." Grief becomes a literal burden we carry.

Gabor Mate, in his book *In the Realm of Hungry Ghosts,* discusses how emotional pain lights up the brain the same way physical pain does. When we hurt, we LITERALLY hurt. It is just as much a bodily burden as a broken bone or serious physical illness.

That's a simple definition of grief. But grief has a habit of never actually being simple. There are different kinds of complicated grief:

- Grief can be *complex,* especially when you experience lots of losses happening close enough together to get all tied together.
- Grief can be *anticipatory*, meaning that we know it is coming so we are hurting every moment until the loss finally happens. And it doesn't hurt any less from all the anticipatory hurting.
- Grief can be *disenfranchised*, meaning that the grief is not recognized in its depth by others in our social network or larger culture. We have cultural rules for the amount of grief we are allowed to feel, don't we? A miscarriage is considered less of a loss than that of a child. A pet is considered less than a person. A neighbor less than a parent. A former partner versus a current one. Grief can also be disenfranchised when the relationship wasn't a healthy one. Sometimes relief is mixed in with that grief which can in turn cause guilt. For example, the loss of a parent who was abusive is often a disenfranchised grief.
- Grief can be *delayed,* meaning that we push it aside and continue to function until the point when it comes back and knocks us sideways. We use busyness as a protective mechanism…until things explode.
- Grief can be *displaced,* meaning we duck and cover on the real source of our grief and have a strong reaction to something else that seems out of proportion. For example, someone may seem stoic at the loss of a parent, then weep uncontrollably after finding a dying bird in their yard some months later.

THE PLATITUDE BULLSHIT PEOPLE SAY THAT DOESN'T HELP

"Time heals everything, you know?"

Fuck yes, I know it will eventually get better. But that's not right now, is it? So stop talking.

"It's a blessing. He was in pain, he was hurting, he was ready to go."

Maybe so. But I wasn't ready. Or maybe I was ready, but now my anticipatory grief just jumped off the high dive. No matter how good a death it was, or how much it had been prepared for, it STILL FUCKING HAPPENED.

"God never gives us more than we can handle."

God (or any higher power) is not some kind of dickhead setting up pain and struggle litmus tests. If She wanted to get my attention or encourage my personal development, there are far better ways to go about it. Things happen to people that they can't handle all the time. That doesn't make us failures in the eyes of our system of faith. Don't short-change anyone's spiritual journey by throwing this in their face, FFS. And don't set them up to feel like they shouldn't ask for help.

"We must be strong."

Why? Why must I? Why can't I be as small, and hurting, and knocked out as I feel? Why am I not allowed my experience? Why do I have to pretend to be better than I feel? Fuck inauthentic strongness. I'm not strong right now so I'm not going to pretend to be.

"You're holding up so well."

This bullshit goes with "being strong." Whether I am or not is besides the point. You have no idea of my private moments or my internal reality. And I don't want to be praised for making everyone around me more comfortable by not wailing and weeping. Because I may need to wail and weep at some point, and now I will be afraid to do so in front of you.

"I know how you feel."

Oh my fucking Buddha, you do NOT. Do not compare your loss to mine. Whether it was less, about the same, or worse. Just don't try to hijack my experience. Everyone's grief is unique. You may have a good idea of what I feel but I promise you do not have the same exact experience as me. Allow me the validity of being the only person who knows exactly what I'm going through at this particular moment.

We've all said this shit and we've all heard this shit. It may not have been offensive to whomever the receiver was, but it certainly wasn't helpful. So please, bite your tongue on the platitudes. If you don't know what to say, just shut the fuck up and be there.

If something stupid slips out, own it. Say "I didn't mean to say something so stupid. I feel awkward and unhelpful and I was trying to come up with something that would make you feel better when there isn't any magical thing to say. I'm so sorry."

Here are some things that you CAN say. None of these statements are magical emotional Neosporin. They may not help. But they won't diminish or demean the grief experience of someone else.

They won't shape or control their behavior to your expectations or social goals.

- You must feel as if this pain will never end.

- I'm so sorry that all this happened to you.

- This must seem like more than you can handle.

- Don't feel that you need to be strong when you are hurting and need help.

- It's OK to cry. Or be mad. Or feel numb. Anything you are feeling is OK.

- Some things just don't make sense.

- I don't have anything to say to make things better for you right now, but I will be here with you.

- I am happy to help in any way I can, but I don't need to do something for you to make myself feel better. I will offer help, but will also not do anything if that's what you prefer.

Or you can *just be quiet*. You don't have to chatter away to be a healing presence in someone's life.

Here are some more ways to care for someone who is grieving.

- Listen differently. Give people space to tell their story if they want. Don't interpret or add your own filter. Show openness and receptivity to what they are saying to show you can be with them as they process. Reflect what they are saying and how they are feeling. Ask open-ended questions that encourage them to continue speaking if they so desire. Validate their experiences. Show that you care and are concerned for them. These are all the basic tricks that therapists use in building relationships with their clients because they are just good *humans connecting to other humans* skills to have.

- Offer specific support that will actually fill a need. Don't make empty, vague offers of support. Sometimes when we are grieving we don't know what would help, but if someone offers to bring the kids to the pool or do the dishes, we realize that would be wonderful.

- Ask what would help. It's also OK to say you don't know what to offer that would actually be helpful, but if there is something that WOULD help you would be happy to do it. If someone else in the grieving person's life is acting as their primary support/point person, ask THEM.

- If they say no, back the FUCK off. Tell them that the offer remains open but don't nag or perseverate.

- Don't expect people to be able to answer questions or make decisions. Avoid asking as much as possible when they are in the first few days of their grief experience. When you feel completely fragmented, pulling the pieces together to be rational feels overwhelming.

- Sit with the person's pain and suffering with compassion. Do this instead of offering positive stories or trying to fix, giving advice or suggestions. Be willing to do nothing, just be with, acknowledge and honor the person, their pain and their suffering. Just having told one's story can often be powerfully therapeutic.

- Attend their story and experience rather than your idea of the truth or what you think they should experience or do.

- Be aware of the bias our culture has toward redemptive stories. Do not try to change, rewrite, reframe or invalidate the person's non-redemptive, non-happy ending stories.

- Give credit for small or large efforts, endurance or strength in facing challenges without being patronizing. If someone is spiraling toward depression, encouragement for the behaviors that are showing movement to healing are important, rather than just rescuing them when they seem overwhelmed.

- Keep one foot in acknowledgment and one in possibilities, but do not insist on always speaking the possibilities.

- Speak to the complexity of the situation, including seeming contradictions. Like, *You can't go on suffering like this AND you don't want to die*. Or, *You want to give up AND you don't want to give up*. The AND statement is infinitely more powerful than a BUT statement. Anytime we preference with a "...but..." we are REALLY saying is "you're wrong" rather than sitting with the contradictions we all feel when grieving.

- Don't forget the forgotten grievers. Oftentimes many people are impacted by a loss, but we focus on certain, primary people.

TAKING ACTION: HONORING GRIEF THROUGH CEREMONY

We've talked about how the human brain is wired for story. And music. And connection. Is it any wonder, then, that we crave ceremony? Cornell anthropologist Meredith Small calls ceremonies *the punctuation marks of life.*

This makes sense, right? If our operating memory can only hold seven (yes, plus or minus two) items of knowledge at a time, is it any wonder, then, that we think in symbols and navigate the world within that reality? That we make meaning through creative expression?

We have certain cultural ceremonies for grief. Funerals being the obvious example. But funerals are often more and more soulless. A box to be checked off, rather than an opportunity to grieve. And so many grief-filled events do not get a closure ceremony. Not because we don't need it, but because there is no language for that need.

And this is where we fill in the gap.

What are you grieving that you don't even have words for? What symbolizes your experience? How can you use these symbols to create meaning? What would your ceremony entail?

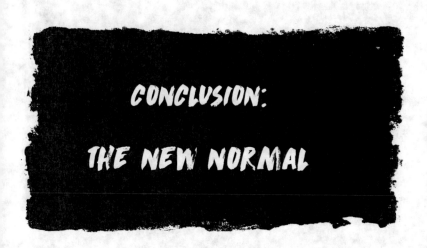

CONCLUSION:

THE NEW NORMAL

Shit gets better. For serious it does. Not perfect, not pre-trauma innocence. But better. And sometimes richer and deeper for the experience of taking back your power on your own terms.

Certain things will probably trigger you. Anniversaries, life circumstances.

But your relationship with your trauma will change. It won't be the beast that controls your every move, anymore.

Your trauma will be more like that pain in the ass neighbor with too much time on their hands.

You know the one.

Who reminds you that the trash pick-up is changed because they are on a holiday schedule. Or tells you that your dog cries a lot when you are at work. Or that the new guy on the floor below totally looks like the drawing of that man that was on the news for robbing a convenience store. You know, *it just might be him.*

They are a well-meaning pain in the ass.

And you make friends with this person the way you do with your trauma.

Sometimes they give you good, useful information. You say thank you. You take the important information and act on it. And you dismiss the rest.

If you don't need to act on it, you tell them thank you for sharing information that is thoughtfully intended to help keep you safe.

You listen, you smile, and you think "Fuck you, Amygdala" and go back to living your life.

RECOMMENDED READING
OTHER PEOPLE WHO WRITE GREAT SHIT

A lot of the books I have found to be helpful over the years tend to have a specific audience that may not intentionally include me or you. Gary Chapman's work on the five love languages is a great example of this. It's a wonderful framework for communicating in relationships, but his books are written from his viewpoint that all romantic relationships are cis-gendered and heterosexual and that Christianity is the standard spiritual practice. None of which is bad if that's your thing, of course. But I mention that as a general warning. A book itself may not be geared towards your identity and life path. But that doesn't mean that the ideas contained therein are worthless. As all of us who don't always fit in have learned...take what works and ignore what doesn't.

Addiction

Memoirs of An Addicted Brain: A Neuroscientist Examines his Former Life on Drugs by Marc Lewis

In The Realm of Hungry Ghosts: Close Encounters with Addiction by Gabor Mate

Eating in the Light of the Moon: How Women Can Transform Their Relationship with Food Through Myths, Metaphors, and Storytelling by Anita A. Johnston

Seeking Safety: A Treatment Manual for PTSD and Substance Abuse by Lisa M. Najavits

A Woman's Addiction Workbook: Your Guide To In-Depth Healing by Lia M. Najavits

Rational Recovery: The New Cure for Substance Addiction by Jack Trimpsey

12 Stupid Things That Mess Up Recovery: Avoiding Relapse Through Self-Awareness and Right Action by Allen Berger

12 Smart Things To Do When The Booze and Drugs Are Gone: Choosing Emotional Sobriety through Self-Awareness and Right Action by Allen Berger

—and all of Patrick Carnes' writings on addiction.

Anxiety, Depression, Anger, and Other Mood Disorders
Hello Cruel World: 101 Alternatives to Suicide for Teens, Freaks, and Other Outlaws by Kate Bornstein

Alive With Vigor! Surviving Your Adventurous Lifestyle by Robert Earl Sutter III

How To Not Kill Yourself: A Survival Guide for Imaginative Pessimists by Set Sytes

Bluebird: Women and The New Psychology of Happiness by Ariel Gore

Maps To The Other Side: The Adventures of A Bipolar Cartographer by Sascha Altman DuBrul

Furiously Happy: A Funny Book About Horrible Things by Jenny Lawson

The Price of Silence: A Mom's Perspective on Mental Illness by Liza Long

Grief

Being With Dying: Cultivating Compassion and Fearlessness in the Presence of Death by Joan Halifax

A Grief Observed by C.S. Lewis

Black Swan: The Twelve Lessons of Abandonment Recovery by Susan Anderson

The Journey from Abandonment to Healing: Surviving Through and Recovering From the Five Stages That Accompany the Loss of Love by Susan Anderson

Sign Posts of Dying by Martha Jo Atkins

Good Grief by Granger E. Westberg

How Can I Help? Reaching Out To Someone Who Is Grieving by June Cerza Kolf

Relationships

Sex from Scratch: Making Your Own Relationship Rules by Sarah Mirk

Consensuality: by Helen Wildfell

How to Be an Adult in Relationships: The Five Keys to Mindful Loving by David Richo

The Five Love Languages by Gary Chapman

—plus Gary Chapman's other relationally specific books that use the love languages model

Self-Compassion
Self-Compassion: The Proven Power of Being Kind To Yourself by Kristen Neff

The Mindful Path to Self-Compassion: Freeing Yourself from Destructive Thoughts and Emotions by Christopher Germer

The Self-Compassion Diet: A Step-by-Step Program to Lose Weight with Loving-Kindness by Jean Fain

Meditation, Mindfulness, and Stress Reduction
Don't Just Do Something, Sit There: A Mindfulness Retreat with Sylvia Boorstein by Sylvia Boorstein

Full Catastrophe Living: Using the Wisdom of Your Body and Mind to Face Stress, Pain, and Illness by John Kabat-Zinn

A Path with Heart: A Guide Through the Perils and Promises of Spiritual Life by Jack Kornfield

—and pretty much everything written by Pema Chodron, Thich Nhat Hahn, and His Holiness The Dalai Lama

Trauma

The Broken Places by Joseph McBride

Dear Sister: Letters From Survivors of Sexual Violence edited by Lisa Factora-Borchers

Trauma and Recovery: The Aftermath of Violence—From Domestic Abuse to Political Terror by Judith L. Herman

—plus everything written by Peter A. Levine

SOURCES
CHAPTERS ONE TO THREE
ALL THE BRAIN AND TRAUMA-WIRING STUFF

Barrett, Lisa Feldman. "Solving the Emotion Paradox: Categorization and the Experience of Emotion." Personality and Social Psychology Review 10, no. 1 (2006): 20–46. Accessed September 7, 2016. doi:10.1207/s15327957pspr1001_2. affective-science.org/pubs/2006/Barrett2006paradox.pdf

Beck, Aaron T. *Prisoners of Hate: The Cognitive Basis of Anger, Hostility, and Violence.* New York: HarperCollins Publishers, 1999.

Beck, Aaron T., John A. Rush, and Brian F. Shaw. *Cognitive Therapy of Depression.* 7th ed. New York: Guilford Publications, 1987.

Beck, Judith S., Aaron T Beck, Judith V. Jordan, and Aaron Carroll. *Cognitive Behavior Therapy, Second Edition: Basics and Beyond.* 2nd ed. New York: Guilford Publications, 2011.

Beck, Judith S and Aaron T Beck. *Cognitive Therapy for Challenging Problems: What to Do When the Basics Don't Work.* New York: Guilford Publications, 2011.

Bush, G. et al. "Dorsal Anterior Cingulate Cortex: A Role in Reward-Based Decision Making. - PubMed - NCBI." 2013. Accessed September 28, 2016. ncbi.nlm.nih.gov/m/pubmed/11756669/

Case-Lo, Christine. "Autonomic Dysfunction | Definition and Patient Education." May 2011. Accessed January 6, 2016. healthline.com/health/autonomic-dysfunction.

Dean, Jeremy. "Anchoring Effect: How The Mind Is Biased by First Impressions." May 23, 2013. Accessed September 3, 2016. http://www.spring.org.uk/2013/05/the-anchoring-effect-how-the-mind-is-biased-by-first-impressions.php.

Foa, Edna B, Terence M Keane, and Matthew J Friedman. *Effective Treatments for PTSD: Practice Guidelines from the International Society for Traumatic Stress Studies.* Edited by Professor Edna B Foa, PhD Terence M Keane, and Executive Matthew J Friedman. New York: Guilford Publications, 2004.

Foster, Jane A. *Gut Feelings: Bacteria and the Brain.* 2013 (July 1, 2013). Accessed September 2, 2016. ncbi.nlm.nih.gov/pmc/articles/PMC3788166/.

Hendy, David. *Noise: A Human History of Sound and Listening.* New York, NY, United States: HarperCollins Publishers, 2013.

Herman, Judith Lewis L. *Trauma and Recovery: The Aftermath of Violence - from Domestic Abuse to Political Terror*. New York, NY: Basic Books, 1992.

Mehl-Madrona, Lewis. *Remapping Your Mind: The Neuroscience of Self-Transformation Through Story*. United States: Bear & Company, 2015.

Miller, George A. *The Magical Number Seven, Plus or Minus Two Some Limits on Our Capacity for Processing Information*. 101, no. 2 (1955): 343–52. Accessed September 3, 2016. psych.utoronto.ca/users/peterson/psy430s2001/Miller%20GA%20Magical%20Seven%20Psych%20Review%201955.pdf.

Mitchell, Jeffrey Diplomate T and American. "TROUSSE PSYCHOTRAUMATIQUE DE DIAGNOSTIC RAPIDE." 2008. Accessed January 4, 2016. info-trauma.org/flash/media-e/mitchellCriticalIncidentStressDebriefing.pdf.

Pessoa, Luiz. "Emotion and Cognition and the Amygdala: From 'what Is It?' to 'what's to Be Done?.'" 2010. Accessed January 4, 2016. lce.umd.edu/publications_files/Pessoa_Neuropsychologia_2010.pdf.

Phelps, Elizabeth. "Human Emotion and Memory: Interactions of the Amygdala and Hippocampal Complex." Current Opinion in Neurobiology 14, no. 2 (2004): 198–202. Accessed May 18, 2016.

Porges, Stephen W. *The Polyvagal Theory: New Insights into Adaptive Reactions of the Autonomic Nervous System*. 76, no. Suppl 2. Accessed June 7, 2016. ncbi.nlm.nih.gov/pmc/articles/PMC3108032/.

Stevens, FL, et al. "Anterior Cingulate Cortex: Unique Role in Cognition and Emotion. - PubMed - NCBI." 2007. Accessed September 28, 2016. ncbi.nlm.nih.gov/m/pubmed/21677237/.

Tulving, Endel. "Episodic and Semantic Memory" (1972). Accessed May 18, 2016. alicekim.ca/EMSM72.pdf.

HJ, Markowitsch and Staniloiu A. "Amygdala in Action: Relaying Biological and Social Significance to Autobiographical Memory. - PubMed - NCBI." 1985. Accessed January 4, 2016. ncbi.nlm.nih.gov/m/pubmed/20933525/.

Judith. "Section 1: Foundations of the Trauma Practice Model 13 6. Tri-Phasic Model (Herman, 1992)." 2005. Accessed January 4, 2016. hogrefe.com/program/media/catalog/Book/trauma-p13-15.pdf.

Junger, Sebastian. *Tribe: On Homecoming and Belonging*. United States: Twelve, 2016.

Lehrer, Jonah. *How We Decide*. Boston: Houghton Mifflin Harcourt, 2009.

Levine, Peter A. *Waking the Tiger: Healing Trauma—the Innate Capacity to Transform Overwhelming Experiences*. Berkeley, CA: North Atlantic Books,U.S., 1997.

Levine, Peter A. and Maggie Kline. *Trauma-Proofing Your Kids: A Parents' Guide for Instilling Joy, Confidence, and Resilience*. Berkeley, CA: North Atlantic Books,U.S., 2008.

Levine, Peter A and Maggie Kline. *Trauma Through a Child's Eyes: Awakening the Ordinary Miracle of Healing: Infancy Through Adolescence*. Berkeley, CA: North Atlantic Books,U.S., 2006.

Levine, Peter A and Gabor Maté. *In an Unspoken Voice: How the Body Releases Trauma and Restores Goodness*. Berkeley: North Atlantic Books,U.S., 2010.

Lipton, Bruce. *The Biology of Belief*. Santa Rosa, CA: Mountain of Love/Elite Books, 2005.

Marsh, Elizabeth & Roediger, Henry. "Episodic and Autobiographical Memory." 2013 Chapter. n.p., 2013. marshlab.psych.duke.edu/publications/Marsh&Roediger2013_Chapter.pdf

Mussweiler, Thomas, Birte Englich, and Fritz Strack. "Anchoring Effect." n.p., n.d. soco.uni-koeln.de/files/PsychPr_04.pdf.

National Center for PTSD "How Common Is PTSD? - PTSD: National Center for PTSD." August 13, 2015. Accessed January 5, 2016. ptsd.va.gov/public/PTSD-overview/basics/how-common-is-ptsd.asp.

Oxford Dictionary. Oxford University Press. s.v "habit: definition of habit in Oxford dictionary (American English) (US)." Accessed January 5, 2016. oxforddictionaries.com/us/definition/american_english/habit.

Oxford Dictionary. Oxford University Press. s.v "post-traumatic stress disorder: definition of post-traumatic stress disorder in Oxford dictionary (American English) (US)." Accessed January 5, 2016. oxforddictionaries.com/us/definition/american_english/post-traumatic-stress-disorder.

Sapolsky, Robert M. *Why Zebras Don't Get Ulcers: An Updated Guide to Stress, Stress-Related Diseases, and Coping*. 3rd ed. New York: W.H. Freeman and Company, 1998.

Schiraldi, Glenn R. *The Post-Traumatic Stress Disorder Sourcebook: A Guide to Healing, Recovery, and Growth*. Los Angeles, CA: McGraw-Hill Professional, 2000.

Taylor, Jill Bolte and Ph. D. Taylor. *My Stroke of Insight: A Brain Scientist's Personal Journey*. New York: Penguin Putnam, 2008.

Trafton, Anne and MIT News Office. "Music in the Brain | MIT News." December 16, 2015. Accessed September 6, 2016. news.mit.edu/2015/neural-population-music-brain-1216.

Treatment Innovations. "All Seeking Safety Studies—Treatment Innovations." Accessed January 4, 2016. treatment-innovations.org/evid-all-studies-ss.html

Turner, Cory. "This Is Your Brain. This Is Your Brain On Music : NPR Ed : NPR." September 10, 2014. Accessed September 6, 2016. npr.org/sections/ed/2014/09/10/343681493/this-is-your-brain-this-is-your-brain-on-music.

Van Der Hart, Onno, Paul Brown, and Bessel A Van Der Kolk. "Pierre Janet's Treatment of Post-Traumatic Stress." 2006. Accessed January 4, 2016. onnovdhart.nl/articles/treatmentptsd.pdf.

Van Der Hart, Onno, Paul Brown, and Horst, Rutger. "The Dissociation Theory of Pierre Janet." 2006. Accessed January 4, 2016. onnovdhart.nl/articles/dissociationtheory.pdf.

Van der Hart, Onno. & Friedman, Barbara "Trauma Information Pages, Articles: Van der Hart Et Al (1989)." January 1930. Accessed January 4, 2016. trauma-pages.com/a/vdhart-89.php.

Van Der Kolk, Bessel. *The Body Keeps the Score: Brain, Mind, and Body in the Healing of Trauma.* United States: Penguin Books, 2015.

Worrall, Simon. "Your Brain Is Hardwired to Snap." News (National Geographic News), February 7, 2016. news.nationalgeographic.com/2016/02/160207-brain-violence-rage-snap-science-booktalk/.

Yahya, Harun. Accessed October 3, 2016. m.harunyahya.com/tr/buku/987/the-miracle-of-hormones/chapter/3689/the-two-governors-of-our-body-the-hypothalamus-and-the-pituitary-gland

CHAPTER FOUR
THE GETTING BETTER THROUGH SELF-CARE STUFF

Bass, Ellen and Jude Brister. *I Never Told Anyone: Writings by Women Survivors of Child Sexual Abuse.* Edited by Louise Thornton. New York, NY: William Morrow Paperbacks, 1991.

Bass, Ellen and Laura Davis. *The Courage to Heal: A Guide for Women Survivors of Child Sexual Abuse.* 3rd ed. New York: HarperPerennial, 1994.

Bounds, Gwendolyn. "How Handwriting Boosts the Brain" - WSJ. (Indiana University), October 5, 2010. wsj.com/articles/SB1000142405274870463150457553193275492518.

Burdick, Debra E and Lcsw Debra Burdick. *Mindfulness Skills Workbook for Clinicians and Clients: 111 Tools, Techniques, Activities & Worksheets*. New York, NY, United States: Pesi Publishing and Media, 2013.

Burns, David D. *When Panic Attacks: The New, Drug-Free Anxiety Therapy That Can Change Your Life*. New York: Crown Publishing Group, 2006.

Culatta, Richard. "Script Theory." 2015. Accessed September 2, 2016. instructionaldesign.org/theories/script-theory.html.

Davis, Laura, Laura Davies, and Laura Hough. *Allies in Healing: When the Person You Love Is a Survivor of Child Sexual Abuse*. New York: William Morrow Paperbacks, 1991.

Domonell, Kristen. "Endorphins and the Truth about Runner's High." January 8, 2016. Accessed September 7, 2016. dailyburn.com/life/fitness/what-are-endorphins-runners-high/.

Domonell, Kristen and Daily Burn. "Why Endorphins (and Exercise) Make You Happy - CNN.Com." CNN (CNN), January 13, 2016. cnn.com/2016/01/13/health/endorphins-exercise-cause-happiness/.

Fischer, Jason B. *The Two Truths about Love: The Art and Wisdom of Extraordinary Relationships*. Oakland, CA: New Harbinger

McMillen, Matt. "Benefits of Exercise to Help With Depression." 2005. Accessed September 7, 2016. m.webmd.com/depression/features/does-exercise-help-depression.

Mazumdar, Agneeth and Jamie Flexman. "5 Brain Hacks That Give You Mind-Blowing Powers | Cracked.Com." March 25, 2013. Accessed August 3, 2016. cracked.com/article_20166_5-brain-hacks-that-give-you-mind-blowing-powers_p4.html.

McMillen, Matt. "Benefits of Exercise to Help With Depression." 2005. Accessed September 7, 2016. m.webmd.com/depression/features/does-exercise-help-depression.

Greenberger, Dennis, Christine A Padesky, and Aaron T Beck. *Mind over Mood: Change How You Feel by Changing the Way You Think*. New York: Guilford Publications, 1995.

Prince Edward Island Rape and Sexual Assault Centre . "Grounding Techniques." 2013. Accessed January 4, 2016. peirsac.org/peirsacui/er/educational_resources10.pdf

Seligman, Martin E. P. *Learned Optimism: [how to Change Your Mind and Your Life]*. 2nd ed. New York, NY: Pocket Books, 1998.

Seligman, Martin E. P. and Seligman Martin. *Authentic Happiness: Using the New Positive Psychology to Realize Your Potential for Lasting Fulfillment*. New York: Simon & Schuster Adult Publishing Group, 2004.

Stahl, Bob and Elisha Goldstein. *A Mindfulness-Based Stress Reduction Workbook.* Oakland, CA: New Harbinger Publications, 2010.

Tennessee Medical Foundation. "Grounding Techniques." Accessed January 4, 2016. e-tmf.org/downloads/Grounding_Techniques.pdf

Williams, Mary Beth, Soili Poijula, Soili Pojula, and Lasse A. Nurmi. *The PTSD Workbook: Simple, Effective Techniques for Overcoming Traumatic Stress Symptoms*. Oakland, CA: New Harbinger Publications,U.S., 2002.

CHAPTER FIVE
TREATMENT OPTIONS AND THE VARIETY OF CARE AVAILABLE

Davis, Joseph A. "Critical Incident Stress Debriefing from a Traumatic Event." February 12, 2013. Accessed January 4, 2016. psychologytoday.com/blog/crimes-and-misdemeanors/201302/critical-incident-stress-debriefing-traumatic-event

EEGInfo.com. "What Is Neurofeedback? FAQ, Watch Video, Find a Neurofeedback Provider in Your Area, Professional Training Courses for Clinicians - EEG Info." Accessed June 7, 2016. eeginfo.com/what-is-neurofeedback.jsp.

Engel, Meredith. "Does Energy Healing Really Work? - NY Daily News." July 18, 2014. Accessed June 7, 2016. nydailynews.com/life-style/health/energy-healing-work-article-1.1872210.

Gelender, Amanda "Doctors Put Me on 40 Different Meds for Bipolar and Depression. It Almost Killed Me. — Invisible Illness — Medium." May 31, 2016. Accessed June 7, 2016. medium.com/invisible-illness/doctors-put-me-on-40-different-meds-for-bipolar-and-depression-it-almost-killed-me-c5e4fbea2816#.cadpk38ga.

International Electromedical Products. "Alpha-Stim Clinical Research." 2016. Accessed June 7, 2016. alpha-stim.com/healthcare-professionals/clinical-research/.

Korry, Elaine. "Too Many Children In Foster Care Are Getting Antipsychotic Meds : Shots - Health News : NPR." September 2, 2015. Accessed June 7, 2016. .npr.org/

sections/health-shots/2015/09/02/436350334/california-moves-to-stop-misuse-of-psychiatric-meds-in-foster-care.

Kubany, Edward S and Tyler C Ralston. *Treating PTSD in Battered Women: A Step-by-Step Manual for Therapists and Counselors*. Oakland, CA: New Harbinger Publications, 2008.

Lieberman, Jeffrey A., T. Scott Stroup, Joseph P. McEvoy, Marvin S. Swartz, Robert A. Rosenheck, Diana O. Perkins, Richard S. E. Keefe, et al. "Effectiveness of Antipsychotic Drugs in Patients with Chronic Schizophrenia — NEJM." New England Journal of Medicine 353, no. 12 (September 22, 2005): 1209–23. doi:10.1056/nejmoa051688.

Mayo Foundation for Medical Education and Research. "Overview - Biofeedback - Mayo Clinic." Mayoclinic January 14, 2016,. Accessed June 7, 2016. mayoclinic.org/tests-procedures/biofeedback/home/ovc-20169724.

Mayo Foundation for Medical Education and Research. "What Is Reflexology? Mayo Clinic." Mayoclinic September 23, 2015,. Accessed September 10, 2016. mayoclinic.org/healthy-lifestyle/consumer-health/expert-answers/what-is-reflexology/faq-20058139.

MentalHelp.net. "Chiropractic Care." 1995. Accessed June 7, 2016. mentalhelp.net/articles/chiropractic-care/.

Miller, Anna. "What Is Reiki? | Health & Wellness | US News." Accessed September 10, 2016. health.usnews.com/health-news/health-wellness/articles/2014/11/10/what-is-reiki

Mitchell, Jeffery. "Critical Incident Stress Debriefing." Accessed January 4, 2016. info-trauma.org/flash/media-e/mitchellCriticalIncidentStressDebriefing.pdf

Najavits, Lisa M. *Seeking Safety: A Treatment Manual for PTSD and Substance Abuse*. New York: Guilford Publications, 2002.

New York State Office Of The Attorney General. "A.G. Schneiderman Asks Major Retailers To Halt Sales Of Certain Herbal Supplements As DNA Tests Fail To Detect Plant Materials Listed On Majority Of Products Tested | Www.Ag.Ny.Gov," 1998, accessed June 7, 2016, ag.ny.gov/press-release/ag-schneiderman-asks-major-retailers-halt-sales-certain-herbal-supplements-dna-tests.

Padesky, Christine A, Dennis Greenberger, and Mark S. Schwartz. *Clinician's Guide to Mind over Mood*. 2nd ed. New York: Guilford Publications, 1995.

Pulsipher, Charlie. "Natural Vs. Synthetic Vitamins – What's the Big Difference?" January 2, 2014. Accessed June 7, 2016. sunwarrior.com/healthhub/natural-vs-synthetic-vitamins.

Quintanilla, Doris. "Chiropractic Care Can Help Lessen Depression Symptoms." December 24, 2013. Accessed September 8, 2016. psyweb.com/articles/depression-treatment/chiropractic-care-can-help-lessen-depression-symptoms.

Rettner, Rachael."Herbal Supplements Often Contain Unlisted Ingredients." Accessed June 7, 2016. livescience.com/40357-herbal-products-unlisted-ingredient.html.

CHAPTERS SIX–TEN
SPECIFIC SYMPTOMS, SITUATIONS, AND DIAGNOSES

Berger, Allen. *12 Stupid Things That Mess up Recovery: Avoiding Relapse Through Self-Awareness and Right Action.* United States: Hazelden Information & Educational Services, 2008.

Blair, R. J. R. *Considering Anger from a Cognitive Neuroscience Perspective.* 3, no. 1. Accessed October 3, 2016. ncbi.nlm.nih.gov/pmc/articles/PMC3260787/.

Carnes, Patrick J. and Ph. D. Patrick. *A Gentle Path Through the Twelve Steps: The Classic Guide for All People in the Process of Recovery.* United States: Hazelden Information & Educational Services, 1994.

Doyle, Robert and Joseph Nowinski. *Almost Alcoholic: Is My (or My Loved One's) Drinking a Problem?* New York, NY, United States: Hazelden Publishing & Educational Services, 2012.

Evans, Katie, Michael J Sullivan, and J. Michael Sullivan. *Dual Diagnosis: Counselling the Mentally Ill Substance Abuser.* New York: Guilford Publications, 1990.

Gulz, Agneta. *Conceptions of Anger and Grief in the Japanese, Swedish, and American Cultures– the Role of Metaphor in Conceptual Processes.* n.p., n.d. lucs.lu.se/LUCS/007/LUCS.007.pdf.

Hamilton, Tim and Pat Samples. *The Twelve Steps and Dual Disorders: A Framework of Recovery for Those of Us with Addiction and an Emotional or Psychiatric Illness.* United States: Hazelden Information & Educational Services, 1994.

Hazelden Publishing. *The Dual Disorders Recovery Book: Twelve Step Programme for Those of Us with Addiction and an Emotional or Psychiatric Illness.* United States: Hazelden Information & Educational Services, 1993.

Hendrickson, Edward L. *Designing, Implementing and Managing Treatment Services for Individuals with Co-Occurring Mental Health and Substance Use Disorders: Blue Prints for Action.* New York: Haworth Press, 2006.

Hahn, Thich Nhat. *Anger: Wisdom for Cooling the Flames.* United States: Riverhead Books,U.S., n.d.

Huesmann, Rowell L. The Impact of Electronic Media Violence: Scientific Theory and Research. 41, no. 6 Suppl 1 (April 12, 2013). Accessed January 6, 2016. ncbi.nlm.nih.gov/pmc/articles/PMC2704015/.

Kubler-Ross, Elisabeth. *On Death and Dying: What the Dying Have to Teach Doctors, Nursers, Clergy and Their Own Families.* New York, NY: Simon & Schuster Adult Publishing Group, 1997.

Lakoff, George and Kovecses, Zoltan. "The Cognitive Model of Anger Inherent in American English" 1983. n.p., 2011. georgelakoff.files.wordpress.com/2011/04/the-cognitive-model-of-anger-inherent-in-american-english-lakoff-and-kovecses-1983.pdf

Lingford-Hughes, Ann and Nutt, David."Neurobiology of Addiction and Implications for Treatment | The British Journal of Psychiatry." EDITORIAL 182, no. 2 (February 1, 2003): 100–197. Accessed October 3, 2016. doi:10.1192/bjp.182.2.97. http://bjp.rcpsych.org/content/182/2/97.

Maté, Gabor. *In the Realm of Hungry Ghosts: Close Encounters with Addiction.* Berkeley, CA: North Atlantic Books, 2011.

Nationmaster. "Japan Vs United States Crime Stats Compared." 2009. Accessed January 6, 2016. nationmaster.com/country-info/compare/Japan/United-States/Crime.

Zwaan, Rolf A. "Experiential Framework for Language Comprehension: The Immersed Experiencer: Toward An Embodied Theory of Language Comprehension." Learning and Motivation 44 (2003) Accessed September 1, 2016. old.nbu.bg/cogs/events/2004/materials/Schmalhofer/Zwaan_2003_learning&motivation.PDF

ACKNOWLEDGEMENTS

When I quit my day job a couple of years back it was to focus on my private practice and write the book I've been wanting to write for years. This was a huge leap of faith for a widow with two kids. And fortunately, everything worked out.

However, this was not the book I intended to write. Go figure.

This book was born, initially, out of me spending fifteen minutes writing down the "five minutes of brain science" talk I have given most of my clients over the years. I sent it to Microcosm Publishing who totally saw the potential in my vaguely formed idea and committed to helping me develop it, which is something publishers just don't do anymore. So the other book is still happening, by the way. Plus we have lots of other cool book ideas brewing. Because in the process, Elly Blue and Joe Biel have gone from being my publishers to my friends. They are brilliant, supportive, and count the number of times I write "fuck" in a manuscript and always suggest a few more. So suck it Dr. Phil…you don't have it nearly so good as I do.

To Aaron Sapp, MD and Allen Novian, PhD, LMFT, LPC-S for being early readers who tried to make sure I didn't embarrass myself on the brain science part. I may have fucked up anyway. Not their fault, of course. Send all hate mail directly to me.

To my son Sammuel, who has been my co-trainer at conferences about brain science and trauma, bravely sharing some of his own stories about losing his father to help others learn.

To my best friend Adrian. Who is always far more successful than all the King's horses and all the King's men. And brings food, on top of that.

To the rest of our crew, because if you don't see your name in print it just doesn't fucking count. Thank you for being my family Shannon, Penny, Brianna, Hailee, Rowan, and Braedan.

To Joe G. Who went from being my boyfriend to my husband in this process. Despite my determination to never get married again. Because (clearly), me getting married is a terrible fucking idea. Unless it's to Joe G. In which case the world starts to make a lot more sense for anyone who knows either one of us.

To my supervisees, past and present. Y'all are so fucking smart and motivated and GOOD at your jobs, I gotta bust my ass to keep up and not embarrass myself. It's the best prevention of epic laziness a girl could ask for!

And finally, to my clients. HOLY SHITBALLZ. You are such bad-ass motherfucking *rock stars* I just can't even wrap my head around how grateful I am to be part of your journey. Thank you for doing all the hard work. And grokking the brain science thing so well that THIS became my first book.

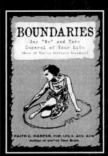

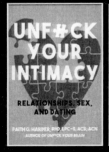
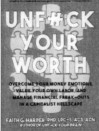
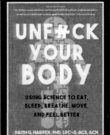